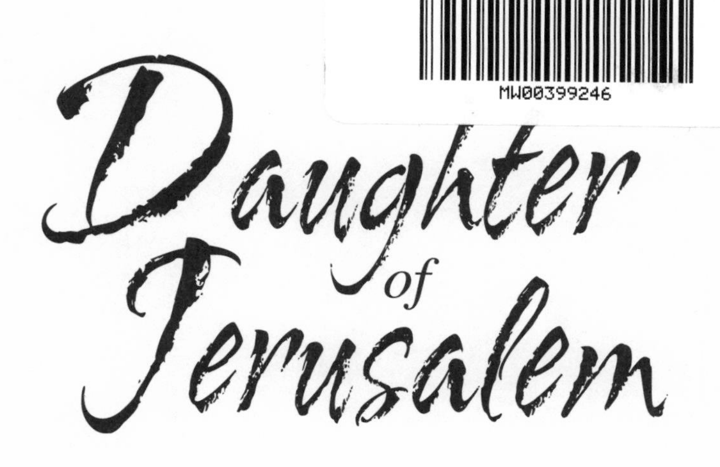

To Suzanne,

May mercy, peace
and love be yours
in abundance. (Jude 2)

Sharon Alice Geyer
2013 Bible Study

Daughter of Jerusalem

An American Woman's Journey of Faith

SHARON GEYER

FaithWalk
PUBLISHING
Grand Haven, Michigan

Published by FaithWalk Publishing
333 Jackson Street, Grand Haven, Michigan 49417

Scripture quotations marked "KJV" are taken from the Holy Bible, King James Version, Cambridge, 1769.

Printed in the United States of America

07 06 05 04 03 02 7 6 5 4 3 2 1

Library of Congress Control Number: 2002115962
ISBN: 0-9724196-2-4 (pbk.: alk. paper)

To Patrick

Who encouraged my writing along the way.
Maybe now he will read it.

Dear Friend

This story is an account of my experiences in the Middle East. My intent has been to relate in narrative form what happened to me, both the sacred and the profane. Although the characters and events are real, certain names have been changed. My account reflects my views and no one else's. My family, friends, and acquaintances may have different interpretations of the same events, and I respect their right to their views. I alone bear responsibility for the substance of what is said in this tale.

Sharon Geyer

Prologue

We spend our years as a tale that is told.

Psalms 90:9 KJV

Los Angeles, 1959

The passport, issued by the Iranian consulate in San Francisco, has a shiny, red plastic cover. The young woman in the grainy black-and-white photograph looks up at the camera with the wistful gaze of an eighteen-year-old. A broad headband holds unruly hair off a face still softened with baby fat. The passport, issued in the name of Fatimah, states her place of birth as simply *abroad.*

The consular clerk in the service of His Majesty, the Shah of Iran, has endowed me with a new identity, and this first encounter with Oriental logic pleases me inordinately. I learn later that Fatimah is the name of the Prophet Mohammed's favorite daughter. Does this clerk assume I'm Muslim? I'm only nominally Christian, so what does it matter? My new in-laws will call me Shareen, which means *sweet* in Farsi.

Equally intriguing is the assignment of a new place of birth. I rather like it, am delighted in fact, by the ambiguity of the word *abroad.* It conjures up endless possibilities. I might have been born in Calcutta, Paris, or even Rangoon. Is this consular clerk able to read the future? Did he foresee the liability of having the United States as one's place of birth?

My passport, in its shiny red cover, is a portent of the dual identity I will live for the next six years in the midst of a Muslim family in Teheran.

As the fourth of six children, the daughter of a milkman and a homemaker, I'm more than ready for adventure, change, anything other than the boring life I've lived in the suburbs of Los Angeles. In this frame of mind, I find it easy to fall in love with a chemistry student from Iran during my freshman year at California State University at Los Angeles.

Mansoor's jet black hair shows a touch of gray at the temples. I notice he loves to show off his handsome profile. His eyes sparkle like black opals under fierce bristling brows. He is slim, graceful, and tall.

I take him to meet my family. My older sister is giving herself a home perm in the kitchen. Mansoor pretends not to notice the cloud of acrid fumes floating into the living room.

"Mom, this is Mansoor." She is sitting in her usual place on the green couch. She nervously straightens the magazines on the coffee table. Mansoor walks over and takes her hand, bowing slightly. *Don't kiss it*, I inwardly plead. He doesn't, but he seems to have won her over. I can see the flush of pleasure on her cheeks.

My father walks in. He is polite, but cool, which doesn't surprise me, Mansoor is thirty years old, and I have just turned eighteen.

On our first date, we go ballroom dancing at a private club. He teaches me to waltz and tango. I'm all elbows and left feet and can't keep time. He thinks he's Fred Astaire and tells me I look like his favorite 1930s movie star, Deanna Durbin. I've never heard of her.

As a child, I had daydreamed that I was a lost princess who was being brought up by this kind milkman and his big family. Now I feel like one.

My parents turn vehemently against our relationship, so we elope after knowing each other only four months. It's 1959, the eve of the 1960s revolution, and I'm getting a jump start on rebellion.

Mansoor insists on buying me a wedding gown and veil, even though a traditional walk down the aisle in a gorgeous gown is not high on my list of priorities. He also arranges for the wedding to take place in the small chapel at the Methodist Church on Wilshire

Boulevard. The minister doesn't know us and doesn't seem to care that neither of us is a member of his church, or even practicing Christians. Mansoor's friend, Nassar, will be the best man. Melinda, my closest friend in high school, will be my maid of honor. No one from my family is invited; however, a few of Mansoor's Iranian friends attend and throw a small party afterwards.

We don't go on a honeymoon, but consummate the union in Mansoor's small studio apartment that night. I'm still a virgin and naive in matters of sex. Even so, I find my first sexual encounter to be a big letdown, considering all the overblown romantic expectations I had. "Is this all there is to it?" I confide later to Melinda. I did, however, produce the "red stain" that verifies my purity and thus satisfied Mansoor's expectations.

In the week following our wedding, Mansoor quit his part-time job at a gas station and also dropped out of school. Now, he can apply for a "green card" and become a permanent resident. I'm sure that he knows what he is doing and will soon get a good job. In the meantime, I take a position as a clerk in an insurance company that pays enough to cover our minimum expenses.

I actually like being a working woman. I sit at a desk between two other young women. One is a petite and elegant Latina. She gets her nails professionally manicured and has her hair set and styled every week. She lives with her parents in nearby East Los Angeles, and they look after her baby. Her husband is in the Marines. The other clerk is plump and pretty, engaged to be married soon. She invites us to her wedding. It's the first Jewish wedding I have attended. It's a first for Mansoor, also. Her wedding reception is a catered affair with hundreds of family and friends. I don't consciously compare my hasty elopement to her well planned affair, but I have to remind myself that I really wanted adventure with Mansoor and that I am very happy.

I become pregnant at age nineteen. Aware of the stigma attached to teenage mothers, I'm relieved that the baby will be born three months after I turn twenty. I buy a new wardrobe, proud to show off the ever increasing bulge in my middle.

Mansoor seems happy but experiences anxiety attacks. His heart races, he can't catch his breath, and he begs me to call emergency. This happens repeatedly, but the doctors can't find anything wrong.

When labor starts, Mansoor takes me to the nearby Queen of Angels Hospital as prearranged. I've read all the books and feel prepared for the ordeal ahead. "It's no worse than bad cramps," was a co-worker's advice. I'm in control the first ten hours. Why didn't anybody warn me it would take so long? My shoulder feels dislocated from violently gripping the bars on the side of my bed. My cracked lips bleed. I give up and admit to myself that I can't and won't make it. Then, a doctor gives me an injection in the spine and I gratefully pass out. I don't know where I am when I hear a voice say, "Here it comes." I sit up to see what's coming just as the doctor catches my baby in his hands. "Oh honey, you will regret doing that," the nurse tells me. How am I to know I'm supposed to lie flat so that the drug doesn't go to my brain? Twenty-four hours later, feeling like a Mack truck rolled over my body, a gentle black nurse gives me a bed-bath, then hands my baby to me. He has a full head of hair, like I did when I was born. I don't have to check each finger and toe. I just know he is perfectly formed.

On the third day, a hospital clerk insists I fill out a birth certificate form. I write Christopher Darius. I think this name is a perfect blend of East and West and I'm sure Mansoor will agree.

"Never," he shouts. "My son must have a name never used by anyone else." His rage startles me, and I quickly acquiesce. He chooses the name Rodwin. Rod is a Persian word and the suffix *win* makes it American but, more importantly, original. I manage to keep Christopher on his birth certificate as a second name.

This marks the beginning of Mansoor's nervous breakdown. He doesn't sleep, loses weight, and can't keep a job. He reluctantly agrees to see a psychiatrist.

The psychiatrist concludes that I am the problem, or at least that is what Mansoor tells me. I don't accept that diagnosis, but it never occurs to me to talk to the doctor directly. I come from a family where seeing a "shrink" is considered an affectation of the idle rich. It is years before I can admit to myself that he is jealous of my position as the mother of our son.

Meanwhile, our life goes on. I return to my job as a typist while he cares for the baby. So begins a long struggle over who will be the "mother" in this family.

When Rodwin is three years old, Mansoor's family sends us tickets to come to Teheran. His mother thinks Mansoor will get well in his own cultural environment. I hope she's right. By now, I'm willing to reinvent my princess fantasy in a new setting.

Part One

If I say, surely the darkness shall cover me;
even the night shall be light about me

Psalm 139:11

Teheran, 1963

As Shareen (no one calls me Fatimah, perhaps in deference to the original Fatimah), I try to fit in with the family living on Alley Fardis, one block off Boulevard Takte Jamshid and one mile from the American Embassy.

My first impression of Teheran is disappointing. It's like stepping into a sepia-colored print or switching from Technicolor to black-and-white with its washed out, faded brown buildings and streets. Even the people wear gray or black clothing. I see no nuances or shades of color. Only after many months can I discern the delicate shades of mauve or pearl gray that abound in a desert landscape.

I learn to search for beauty in the secret Persian gardens hidden behind drab clay walls. I peer over shoulders, as a man or woman enters a private gate, to catch a glimpse of water fountains flowing over turquoise tiles. I see rose bushes with blooms as large as cabbage heads. I'm desperately trying to keep my princess illusion alive.

Teheran's brutally hot summers force us to sleep on the flat rooftop to catch the night breeze. The metal beds, draped with gauzy mosquito netting, look like derelict sailing vessels.

Families who can afford it build a second home on the slopes of the nearby Alborz Mountains. It's always cool there in summer, where the mountain streams irrigate the private gardens. Mansoor's family doesn't own a home in the foothills, but at least we often picnic there.

These picnics are all-day affairs with lamb kebab over steamed rice, followed by hot sweet tea from a Russian samovar. The men change into pajama bottoms to protect the crease in their good trousers. Children splash in the snow-fed stream while their mothers keep a careful eye on them.

One

My princess fantasy begins to crack, as I admit my Persian palace is a ramshackle old house made of clay bricks. When Mansoor's father had it built fifty years ago, he considered it spacious and innovative because of the brick oven and grill in the kitchen. It even had its own bathhouse, or *hammam*.

To my American eyes, the house is wanting the minimum of modern conveniences. The toilet is a closet with a hole in the cement floor, and it stinks. A small water can with a long spout, like the one I use to water house plants, sits under a water spigot. This replaces toilet paper. I can't squat without losing my balance, so Mansoor has a carpenter build a wooden stool for me to sit on. When I pee, it splatters my legs, so I shove it in the corner and learn to squat by holding the water spigot for balance.

Friday mornings, my mother-in-law lights the kerosene heater in the hammam for the communal bath. All the women in the house crowd in to bathe, wax their legs, dye their hair with henna, drink tea, and eat oranges. Mama Badri calls me to join them.

"I've already bathed," I shout back through the closed door, hoping they won't insist. My American modesty won't allow me to bathe with others, even if it is just women and children.

A village woman comes to do the laundry. She is thin with stringy arm muscles and rough hands like a man's. Her front teeth are large like a camel's. She removes her *chador*, or veil, when she starts to work, revealing a flouncy cotton dress worn over pantaloons. I've got a pile of dirty laundry building up in the corner of our bedroom. Where and how she is going to do the laundry, I don't know. I find no laundry room in the house or in the outside storerooms.

Fascinated, I watch as she builds a wood fire in the courtyard. Then she places a large tin tub over the fire, fills it with pitchers of water, and throws in the dirty laundry. Using a block of white soap, she vigorously scrubs the clothes by hand, rinses once, and wrings the water out by violently twisting each garment into a pretzel shape. I don't see any clothesline, but I follow her as she carries the clothes to the front garden and drapes them on any convenient bush or tree.

That night, I ask Mansoor why he doesn't put up a clothesline. He replies with a knowing nod that implies I'm simple minded. "A thief can jump over the seven-foot wall and steal it in the night."

After two months of this treatment, most of our American-made clothes resemble limp rags. To salvage what I can of our wardrobe, I take over the laundry, washing them in a tub of hot water in the hammam during my weekly shower. At least I have a kerosene stove to heat the water.

Used to a quick daily shower in the United States, I find the once-a-week hammam ritual exhausting but surprisingly adequate. The tiled hammam is hot, and I sit on a little stool and let the steam penetrate every pore in my body. Then I soap up with a stiff cloth made of camel hair that sloughs the dead skin cells off in a gray roll. This never happens in a quick shower. Then I rinse with warm water and suds up again. After several applications, I finish with a cool water rinse.

The family compound contains a curious mixture of odors and fragrances that entice and repel me simultaneously. The sweet smells of ripe mulberries permeate the garden. In the kitchen, kerosene fumes vie with the smell of onions and garlic frying in some kind of pungent fat.

"What's Mama Badri cooking with?" I ask as I wrinkle my nose.

"Sheep's fat," Mansoor replies. "Only Persian sheep have these large, flat tails full of perfumed fat."

Every dish on the table, except the yogurt and salad, is cooked in this oil. It gags me. I'm going to die of starvation, I moan to myself. Later, as my taste buds adjust, I'm able to screen out the *perfume* and enjoy the delicate flavors of dill or saffron mingled with the rice.

Contrary to all the cliches of the overbearing mother-in-law, Mama Badri is an angel in polyester. She wears her thinning gray hair in long braids covered with a polyester scarf (tradition requires the chador only in the presence of a mullah).

She keeps her home immaculately with no modern appliances, except a refrigerator, and cooks on two kerosene burners. Every morning, after her early prayers and a glass of hot tea, she chops onions, garlic, and various vegetables for the midday stew. Then she carefully steams one kilo of rice in a large kettle, covered with a lid bound in cloth like a pillow to catch the steam.

My sister-in-law is a short, stout woman with a beautiful complexion and a mouth shaped like a rosebud. She resents me for several good reasons: She and her husband had to vacate their bedroom for the three of us (they now sleep in the family room); I can't pronounce her name properly (it always comes out close to the Farsi word for grasshopper); and I take the best piece of meat, small as it is, and put it on Rodwin's plate. I'm afraid he is not getting enough protein, but I worry in vain. He will grow to be a head and shoulders taller than other children his age.

I try to ingratiate myself with my mother-in-law, correctly guessing that she will be my only ally in this household. Nothing disturbs her calm nature, even when I inadvertently defile her laundry. The sky turned dark and, before the rain poured down, I pulled Mama Badri's clothes off the bushes and placed them on her bed. How am I to know it's forbidden for a non-Muslim to touch the undergarments of a believer?

"You are ceremonially *najest*, or unclean," Mansoor explains. "Now Mama Badri will have to wash her laundry again."

Just as he predicted, she came home, inquired who had brought in her laundry, and washed them again when she heard it was Shareen. But she never said a word to me.

Almost daily I have to learn about cultural and religious customs and taboos. Most of the time I learn by doing it wrong. I also learn about Mansoor's father's method of child discipline when Mansoor tells me stories about his childhood in this house. For example, when he was eleven years old and his brother two years older, they liked to tell jokes while they sat under the *corsi*, or heater. With their feet snuggled up against the charcoal brazier and the quilt pulled to their chests to keep themselves warm during the cold winter evenings, the brothers would tell each other jokes.

Mansoor cracked dried watermelon seeds between his front teeth and laughed at his brother's joke about what goes on between men and women. Mansoor sat with his back to the door and did not see the shadow announcing his father's presence.

"Like this?" Mansoor giggled, making a circle with the forefinger and thumb of his left hand. Then with a stiff forefinger he jabbed obscenely through the hole.

Mansoor's laughter died on his lips as his father's strong hand grabbed the back of his collar. Calling him a piece of camel dung, his father dragged him out of the sitting room and down the hall to the kitchen. Mama Badri stood with a puzzled look on her round, smooth face while her husband locked Mansoor in the pantry.

Terrified and claustrophobic in the narrow, dark room, Mansoor choked on the pungent smell of pickles in clay jars. To this day he won't eat anything pickled. He climbed on to a gunny sack of rice to pull aside the gauze curtain covering the window in time to see his father removing his clothing.

He carefully took off his dark blue wool jacket, folded it, and placed it on a kitchen chair. Then he stripped off the white shirt (worn only to his office) and the matching trousers. Standing in his striped shorts and sleeveless undershirt, he commanded his wife to bring a towel and the heavy knife used for chopping meat.

Mansoor saw the clenched teeth and the black eyebrows bristling in one continuous line. His father meant to butcher him like a sacrificial goat. His mother stood wild eyed and shaking with fear. Mansoor watched mesmerized as his father tied the towel around his waist and balanced the long, sharp blade in the palm of his hand.

Then Mama Badri opposed her husband for the first and only time in her life. "Kill me first," she said, her determined soul glittering in her eyes.

His father dropped the butcher knife and stomped to his bedroom without a word. Mama Badri fell to her knees in the pile of his discarded clothing. Mansoor crashed to the floor in a faint, knocking a jar of quince jam off the shelf.

After hearing this story I feel revulsion toward my dead father-in-law. Every time I look at his photograph sitting in the place of honor on the marble mantle, I silently curse him.

I have accepted the dual citizenship premise, believing it worked both ways. Now I find that from the official Iranian point of view, I'm a citizen of their country exclusively and must abide by their laws. I'm pragmatic, and I try to adapt to my new circumstances. First, I must master the formal social manners.

"You embarrass me when you say good-night to guests in the foyer, before they say good-bye first," Mansoor complains. "It looks as if you are trying to rush them out."

"Stand up when an older person enters the room, but never stand for someone your own age and, for God's sake, don't greet the laundry woman as if she is an invited guest. Refuse twice before accepting the offer of cakes or sweets."

At social occasions when I'm left out because of the language barrier, I make a pig of myself out of pure boredom. I stay skinny, never-the-less, eating sugar coated almonds, thick gelatinous Turkish delight studded with pistachios, and something with the horrible name of *gazz*, which melts in my mouth like salt water taffy. I've learned to peel an orange or apple in one long continuous peel, arrange it to resemble a carved rose and hand it to my hostess. When tea, served in miniature glasses with tiny silver spoons, is offered for the third time, I sigh with relief, knowing it's time to leave.

In thanksgiving for the return of her son from America, Mama Badri prepares a feast for the female relatives only. After two days of preparation in the kitchen, she places a long white tablecloth on the carpet in the formal, seldom-used guest room.

Mama Badri brings in platters of savory rice with dill and lima beans, sweet rice with candied orange peel or dried cherries, plates of roasted chicken and lamb, clay bowls of yogurt, plates of fresh mint, white cheese, and flat bread.

She places it all in a strategic arrangement so that no guest has to reach more than a few inches. Now, I understand why *please pass*, is not in their vocabulary. It's simply not necessary.

A mullah is coming to recite prayers before the feast begins, so I must wear a chador. Mama Badri hands me a rectangular piece of cloth the size of a twin bed sheet. This one is black, but they come in all colors, including white with printed flowers. I awkwardly drape it over my head and body so just my face is showing. It has no fastener, so I learn the trick of holding it together under my chin with my free hand. If necessary, I clamp the two sides together with my teeth.

The turbaned mullah sits at the head of the carpet and recites in a high sing-song voice. Then, without warning the women wail and sob in great heaving bursts, pulling their chadors across their faces for privacy.

I tense up but don't know how to react. As wild animals freeze when something momentous is about to happen, I don't move a muscle. Very slowly, I feel myself being pulled into the group hysteria. I'm working up to an outburst of tears when abruptly the crying stops. The mullah stands, then exits the room. Too stunned to speak, with unshed tears pounding against my eyelids, I look around in confusion.

Before the black-robed priest reaches the garden gate, the ladies toss back their veils (revealing an abundance of gold jewelry and plenty of makeup) and begin eating with unabashed enthusiasm. I can hardly eat as the food sticks in my throat. Later, in private, I ask Mama Badri what prompted the hysterical burst of grief among the women.

"The mullah recited the tragedy of Imam Hussein's martyrdom and death, and it touched each woman's personal sorrows," she replies.

"Hussein?" I ask. I've never heard of him but don't want to let on to my ignorance.

"Hussein, the prophet's true heir, fought the Sunni usurpers until his blood colored the desert sand bright red."

I listen intently as Mama Badri gives me a history lesson about the treachery between Sunni and Shi'ite branches of Islam.

"According to Mohammed there were four perfect women: Asiyah, the wife of Pharaoh; Mary, the mother of Jesus; Khadija, his first wife; and his favorite daughter, Fatima. Fatima married Ali and had two sons, Hassan and Hussein. Hassan's descendants are called Sheriffs, or nobles. Seyyed, or lord, is the title of Hussein's male descendants. The line of succession to the Caliphate is from these two sons, no other. This is where we diverge from the Sunni.

"Why are you called Shi'ites?"

The word Shi'a means a party, as in partisans of Ali. The Sunni thought they could elect a successor to Mohammed, so they killed Hussein. We shall continue to mourn him unto the very bosom of Paradise. The heart of every true Shi'a is the living tomb of Hussein."

"Are you talking about the tenth of Muharram?" I ask, remembering that Mansoor warned me not to go outside the compound on this day. "Men will beat themselves bloody with clubs and chains in memory of Hussein's death," he told me with distaste.

He didn't seem to share Mama Badri's veneration of this holy man.

I am pleased to meet another foreign bride at the feast. Barbara is German and married to a close family friend. She takes me aside and, speaking in good English, says, "You are nothing like we expected."

"What do you mean?" I answer, puzzled but happy to find someone who speaks English.

"Mansoor wrote letters describing you as a mean bitch." She giggles, whether out of nervousness or embarrassment, I don't know.

I have no words to reply. I feel that Mansoor has betrayed me in the worst way. My chest hurts and I can't breathe. With sudden clarity I realize that I don't know the man I married. I can't fathom how or, even worse, why, he has this hatred towards me. We've had our differences, but nothing that would indicate the depth of his contempt for me.

"Come over for tea one afternoon," Barbara says. "We will be friends, and my children will play with your son and learn English."

We do become friends, and I admire her blonde beauty and German tenacity. She keeps her husband on a tight rein, threatening to leave him to raise their children alone if he doesn't please her. It works for her, but intuitively I know that I can't pull off any such thing.

From the day of the feast, and my new awareness of Mansoor's twisted mental state, I am a different person. I feel I am hated without cause. I also know I am virtually a prisoner. Any change in my immediate circumstances will have to be an inner change, a spiritual journey, so to speak.

I know I should never have left the United States. If only I had listened to my father's warnings. I have bitter regrets and only myself to blame. Many evenings I sit alone in the garden and silently cry. As I look up at the myriad stars I plead for help, even though I don't believe in a personal God who answers prayer. Irrationally, I cry out to my grandmother, who died the same year I was born. "If you are up there, Grandma, please help me."

I have few preconceived ideas or even a logical guide for this journey. Offhand, I reject the Christian ideas that I absorbed by osmosis while growing up. I tried them and they failed, or so I think.

I start with Islam, although, with the exception of Mama Badri, no one in the household is a practicing Muslim. Only she rises before dawn and faces Mecca on a prayer mat.

"Tell me about God," I say, washing the dishes while she sweeps the floor after dinner. I actually use the word Allah, not God, because I'm speaking in my broken Farsi.

"Talk to my brother, Nosrollah," she replies without looking up. "He's an educated man who translates religious tracts from Arabic to Farsi."

Uncle Nosrollah turns out to be a kind old man (decency and strong character seems to flow on Mama Badri's side of the family, as opposed to Mansoor's father's side). He is tall, thin, clean shaven with thick white hair, a religious scholar, not a mullah. He wears a business suit, no turban. We sit in the living room with a bowl of pistachios on the table between us.

First he tells me about the obligation to visit Mecca.

"It is every Muslim's duty to perform the *haj*, or pilgrimage, at least once in his or her life, if they are physically and financially able to. The pilgrims abstain from perfumes, cosmetics, jewelry, and wear a white garment. The haji must abstain from sex, argumentation, fighting, killing of plants and animals, he does not cut his hair or nails, and he does not wear a sown garment."

"Has Mama Badri been to Mecca?" I am curious because I get the impression she has never traveled outside Iran.

"No, my dear Shareen. My sister is not a haji. It has always been her wish to go to Karbala in Iraq, where Hussein was martyred. But for political reasons, that is not an option. So now, most women like my sister choose to travel to Imam Reza's tomb in Mashhad."

Uncle Nosrollah goes on about the minutiae of religious rites, such as ceremonial cleansing of the hands, feet, and lips before prayer. There is a prayer to be said upon wakening in the morning, a prayer to be said on entering and leaving the toilet, the prayers of ablution.

"When standing raise your hands so high the whiteness of your armpits can be seen. Then one must wipe one's face with the hands at the end of supplication. Like this." He demonstrates for me.

"There is a right way and a wrong way to purify the dishes or laundry," he continues.

I'm grateful he says nothing about my blunder with Mama Badri's underwear, if indeed he had even heard about it.

"There is a prayer for when entering the mosque, another one for a new garment, or an evil omen. *Oh God, no one brings good things but you, and no one takes away evil things but you.*

"*Praise be to God, who has given moderation and uprightness to my person, and has given nobility and beauty to the form of my face, and to Him who has made me one of the Muslims.*"

"But, Uncle, tell me what you *personally* know about God," I plead.

"*God*?" His bushy white eyebrows go up. "Shareen, my dear, I know nothing *personally* about God. Perhaps a mullah can tell you something about God."

I'm keenly disappointed, but I try to hide it. If a pious man like Uncle Nosrollah doesn't have any firsthand knowledge of God, I will have to look elsewhere.

I don't conduct my search in any systematic manner. Rather I observe people to see if they have that quality of inner peace that I lack. The family next door are Bahai, a religion that combines Christian, Jewish, and Muslim dogma. We often hear these neighbors quarreling. One day the teenage daughter's screams and shrieks pierce the quiet of the alley.

"Get the police!" I shout to Mansoor as I run next door, taking the staircase two steps at a time. As I burst through the unlocked door, I see the father pounding his stepdaughter's head on the tiled floor. Mansoor arrives with a placid-looking policeman. No charges are filed and the neighbors never speak to us again. By this time, I am not surprised and not even outraged at the official reaction to abuse of women.

But, I scratch Bahai off my mental list, even though I know this is not an objective test case. In my philosophy, one strike and you're out.

Next, I focus my search on Mansoor's best friend. He and his wife belong to the small Zoroastrian community in Teheran. I know this was the official religion of Persia before the Arabs from surrounding lands conquered and imposed Islam. I know little else about their beliefs other than their concept of cosmic Good and Evil.

The next time we go out to dinner together for *juju-kebab*, tender young chicken (the only food Mansoor thinks is safe to eat in a restaurant because it is grilled in view of the customer), I ask them to tell me about their religion.

"Let me explain what happens when a Zoroastrian dies," begins this pleasant, well educated man.

"The corpse is carried out into the desert and placed in an open burial tower built for this purpose. Vultures gather and pick the flesh off the bones. Months later the clean bones are interred in the earth."

I manage to finish my meal. By now I am skilled at disguising my feelings, but I will always associate tiny chicken drumsticks with vulture pickings.

Then I meet Jim and Roberta. Jim is an American entrepreneur who owns Teheran's first hamburger restaurant and mini-golf course. His Iranian partner is Mansoor's friend from high school.

Roberta raises five little towheads who can speak Farsi like the locals. She invites Mansoor and me to their home on Thanksgiving. I am eager for American friendship even if Mansoor is not. When Roberta serves turkey, with all the fixings except cranberry sauce, I have second helpings of everything.

After dinner, as we sit in their comfortable living room, I admire their beautiful beige tribal carpets.

Mansoor whispers in my ear in a disdainful tone, "Americans always prefer the simpler and cheaper carpets."

It's true. I've noticed that his family saves and sacrifices to buy expensive carpets in intricate designs of red and blue.

"We can't afford either kind," I reply.

One of the other invited guests, an American, stands and informally shares how he came to believe in Jesus Christ. Mansoor, deeply offended, hisses in my ear, "I will never return here." Of course, he is extra polite to Roberta and Jim, thanking them profusely when it is time to leave. "*Ghorbaneh shoma*, I sacrifice myself for you. *Koochekeh shoma hastam*, I am your little one, *nocaretam hastam*, I am your servant."

In turn, Jim, well versed in *taroff*, the eloquent custom of formal manners, replies "*ghadamet ruyeh cheshmam*, your footsteps are on my eyes, or you're always welcome in my home."

Christmas passes without celebration, and then Roberta invites me to a ladies-only Bible study. By now I am desperate for the companionship of English-speaking women. In Roberta's home I meet other foreign wives like myself, wives of American oilmen or businessmen, and a few missionaries.

The Bible study, however, annoys me. We are reading from the book of Samuel. A woman called Hannah desperately wants a son but can't conceive. What do I care about this Jewish woman who lived more than two thousand years ago? It is not relevant to my life. I'm a prisoner in this country, my home life is getting worse, we're running out of money, and I can't find God. But I keep attending because I miss hearing and speaking English.

Roberta serves an elaborate tea party after the Bible study. Her dining room table is covered with homemade pies, cookies, and cakes, along with pots of tea and flasks of coffee. I enjoy the chitchat in English as I fill my plate with goodies.

At my in-laws' house on Alley Fardis, I'm left out of conversations because I still speak broken Farsi. Rodwin is doing better in picking up Farsi, or so I think, until his preschool teacher asks me what language he speaks at home.

"Farsi with relatives and servants. English with me," I reply. Her question puzzles me. I ask her what language Rodwin speaks at school.

"I've never heard him say a word in either language."

That surprises me because he loves to recite the poems and songs he learns in her class. He stands at attention in front of me, his arms hanging straight at his side, speaking in a melodious sing-song voice, "*Yek toup daram, ghare-gheli*—I have a little round ball."

Mansoor still has difficulty finding and keeping a job, so, once again, financial necessity compels me to find work. A friend tells me that the United Nations Development Program needs an English-speaking clerk.

A Greek with the name of Pappadopoulos interviews me. He hires me as an assistant in the finance office. My department consists of a Muslim, an Armenian, an Iraqi Jew, and now an American. The UN matches the funds put up by the local government, and the Shah is generous. All employees have a car and driver, even a low-level clerk like me. My driver arrives every morning at 7:30. If I occasionally need to work past 1:30 P.M., I send him to the kindergarten to pick up Rodwin.

I'm at my desk by 8:00 A.M. The tea boy (actually an old man) delivers hot glasses of tea in the finance office. Marina picks up the phone, calls her driver, and asks him to go to a nearby bakery and get us fresh pastries.

Mr. Pappa, as he is affectionately called by his staff, is reading the Teheran *Journal*, an English daily. "Listen to this girls," he says. We look up from our desks only mildly interested.

"The Majlis has enacted a new law that decrees the first wife must be consulted before the husband can take a second or third wife."

We all stop what we are doing. The only sound in the room is the newspaper crackling as Mr. Pappa folds it in half.

"Also," he pauses for dramatic emphasis, "Women in Iran now have the right to initiate a divorce."

"Something I don't have to worry about because Mansoor can't support one wife, let alone two or three," I wisecrack. I'm excited to learn that women have the right to initiate a divorce, but I don't want to show it.

"We can thank Empress Farah for these new laws," responds Mahin, the only Muslim in the office. She and her husband are separated, and he has custody of their only child.

"How is Farah responsible?" asks Marina, who is single but dating one of the married men in the UN.

"When the Prime Minister died recently, two wives and their children showed up for the funeral. The first wife is Farah's friend. She had a nervous breakdown when she discovered her husband had a secret second family." Mahin knows all the royal gossip.

At last, I see a way out of my miserable marriage. I will be one of the first women in Iran to initiate a divorce. The very next day, I ask my UN driver to take me to the courthouse instead of the office. He does as I ask him and, because I can't read or write in Farsi, I ask him to fill out the forms requesting a divorce.

A month later, Mansoor receives his summons to appear in family court. I also must attend. I am nervous but determined to have my day in court.

We enter a plain room with three or four folding chairs facing a desk. An overhead fan hums like it needs lubrication. The judge looks up and motions us to sit. He silently reads the papers on his desk, then takes off his glasses and looks intently in our direction. I involuntarily hold my breath.

"I am deeply disturbed that you (he glares at Mansoor) have not held a steady job in years. This is a disgrace. Under Muslim law, any money the wife makes is hers exclusively."

Mansoor shoots an angry look my way. I slowly exhale, pleasantly surprised by the judge's fairness. I never expected Islamic law to defend me in this way.

"Go to work, come home at the end of the day, and eat what is set before you," says the judge.

This last admonition is in reference to Mansoor's written counter-claim that all I cook is eggs.

"We want to keep families together. Try for six months. If it doesn't work out, come back and I will grant a divorce." The judge nods in my direction.

I walk out of the courthouse with mixed feelings. I am disappointed that the divorce was not granted, but at the same time I feel elated that the judge took my side. I can wait another six months, confident that Mansoor won't have a steady job.

By the end of six months, I find I'm pregnant again. I know the marriage is over. Nevertheless, the pregnancy induces feelings of well-being. The newly created life in my womb produces a sense of hope. I imagine women have felt like this throughout the ages; hoping against all odds that things will turn out well.

The UN gives me a generous six months paid maternity leave. "That would never happen in America," I tell my colleagues. They look skeptical. The wealthiest nation on earth is stingy? They can't believe it.

My obstetrician comes highly recommended and owns his own hospital for women. The Shah's sister is said to be his patient, which is the highest endorsement in the land.

"It's time," I tell Mansoor when the contractions are five minutes apart. He drives me to the hospital, then I tell him to go home, remembering his nervous condition at Queen of Angels in Los Angeles.

After I am given the customary enema, the nurse directs me to the only European-style toilet in the hospital. Iranians rarely use these Western-style toilets, and the plumbing seldom works. More times than I care to remember, a hostess has graciously led me to a modern bathroom. Too late, I find there is no water in the toilet tank.

Now there is plenty of water, I note with mounting horror, as the toilet overflows onto the floor and down the corridor. In the last stages of labor, I do what I have to do. I stagger around the corner and use the "hole in the floor" facility.

Back in bed, I keep a stiff upper lip as Westerners are prone to do. Up and down the corridor, I hear Iranian women screaming without inhibition. The nurse takes my silence to mean the labor is slowing down and doesn't check on me for hours. Later, when she finds me in full dilation, she pages the doctor, decides there is no time to wait for a gurney, and pulls me barefoot down the hall in a desperate attempt to get to the delivery room before the doctor.

On the delivery table, I obsess about the dirty soles of my feet staring the doctor in the face. But I forget my bare feet when a nurse leans over and presses on my huge belly.

"Push!" she exhorts.

I abandon the fortitude of my Anglo ancestors and join my Iranian sisters with a scream that won't stop even when they put the oxygen mask on my face.

The new baby is a strong little fellow, with the same full head of beautiful hair like his brother. Tiny scars on his face and arm look like a string of miniature pearls that broke in the amniotic fluid and landed gracefully on his delicate skin. This time I leave the choice of name to Mansoor. I'm thankful that he doesn't like the popular custom of naming a male child Ali-Reza, Mohammed-Ali, Reza-Mohammed or some variation on that theme.

Mansoor takes his time naming the baby because he wants an original name for his second son, just like he did with Rodwin. In the meantime, we call the baby *Dadash*, baby brother. Dadash reaches his first birthday with no official name or birth certificate.

This bothers my Western sensibilities, but seems entirely reasonable to my in-laws.

As our son's second birthday approaches, an elderly aunt, bent double with age, pays us an unexpected visit.

"His name is *Shad*," she declares with authority that only age confers.

Shad, meaning joy, sounds agreeable to his father. He tacks on the suffix "win," making it Shadwin. I mentally add Timothy as a second name. Shadwin Timothy. I like the sound of it. I'm hoping it's a portent of good things to come for a child conceived in sorrowful circumstances.

Before I return to my job at the United Nations, (with all thought of divorce now on hold) I must hire a nanny for the baby. An aunt brings over an old village woman.

"She eats opium. Addicts don't eat much and therefore are cheap to maintain," she reassures me.

I forbid this nanny to go near the baby and send her away the following morning. The next one I hire is younger but spends hours visiting with her boyfriend at the corner vegetable shop. I eventually hire a nanny recommended by colleagues at the UN.

Khadija, named after the Prophet's first wife, not only takes good care of the baby, but cooks, cleans and efficiently organizes the household. She is an intelligent but uneducated woman, born in Azerbaijan, near the Russian border.

When Mansoor makes a rare appearance for the mid-day meal, Khadija eats alone in the kitchen. On the days when he dines at his mother's or his sister's house, Khadija eats with me in the dining room and we talk about our children. She always cooks enough rice and stew so that there are leftovers to take home for her own children.

When Mansoor fires her (for eating too much), I fear that he will try to be the child-care provider again.

Now desperate, I write to my mother to ask for help in getting out of Iran. It humbles me to admit my situation to her, but by now my pride is shattered. She writes to her U.S. senator, who in turn contacts the American Embassy in Teheran. In due time, the Consular General calls me in and explains that there is nothing he can do because I am officially an Iranian citizen.

"We have file cabinets full of cases like yours." His tone of voice implies that he is sympathetic but powerless.

"What would you have done if my husband had accompanied me on this visit?" I don't think this man appreciates the danger I'm in.

"In that case, my dear, I would speak about some inconsequential paperwork concerning your passport."

I smile weakly. I'm not comforted, but at least he understands.

"Your father has airline tickets waiting for you at the local TWA office, if that's any consolation."

That is comforting, good old Dad. But I know that finding a way to use the tickets will be another matter. Travelers leaving Iran through Mehrabad Airport must report to the police forty-eight hours in advance. The Shah's government doesn't allow anyone to leave the country without a security check. Plus, as a woman, I will need written permission from my husband. I don't know if I will ever be able to use the tickets, but at least I know they're waiting for me at the airline office.

Through American friends, I meet a U.S. Air Force pilot who is willing to smuggle me out on a U.S. military plane, but he will not risk taking my boys.

Another friend introduces me to someone who could take me to the northern border between Iran and Russia. This plan entails our hiking alone through miles of wolf-infested mountains in hopes of finding a Russian patrol. I can't imagine putting my boys in such danger.

Then a Peace Corps volunteer tells me about a German man who can get us across the border to Pakistan. I agree to meet him.

Three days before the planned escape, I attend Bible study as usual. Before the afternoon is over, Roberta looks straight in my eyes and says, "Whatever you're planning, don't do it." She speaks with such authority that I wince.

How could she possibly know? I had confided in no one. Is this God warning me? I learn much later that this German would have used me and my children to smuggle drugs across the border. If caught, I would have spent many years in jail. Shaken but relieved to have avoided this disaster, I put aside any plans for escape.

At the end of the Bible study meeting, we usually stand in a circle, holding hands for a final prayer. This day the women begin to sing instead of pray. Each voice is blending a different melody with exquisite harmony. I don't recognize the words or the music, so I open my eyes to see who is orchestrating this angelic choir, but they all have their eyes shut. The music stops as mysteriously as it began. Everyone says good-bye and goes home.

Curious, I linger to ask Roberta some questions. "Where did you learn to sing like that and when do you get together to practice?"

"Holy Spirit," she mumbles, sounding embarrassed.

This invisible choir director bothers me because it raises serious questions. I remind myself that I'm coming for the friendship only. My spiritual search couldn't possibly end in the claims of Jesus Christ. Isn't this what I rejected when I married a Muslim? I thought I knew what Christianity had to offer and found it lacking. Yet, something spurs me to ask more questions.

I ask Roberta the same question I asked Uncle Nosrollah. "What do you personally know about God?"

I can't recreate her answer, no matter how hard I try, but she says enough to convince me that she is on a first-name basis with God Almighty. I leave her house deeply disturbed.

The months pass and Mansoor is now calling me a *sonofabitch* American in front of the children. True to my passive/aggressive nature, I say nothing, but feel murder in my heart. At the same time, I sense I'm on the verge of a spiritual breakthrough.

In theory, salvation means transformation. But I'm not experiencing a positive transformation. On the contrary, violent, murderous impulses flood my waking thoughts.

"I will stab him over and over with a knife," I confess to my friend Alice, as we walk home from our afternoon of tea and scripture. "A gun is too impersonal. I want to use my hands."

Alice says nothing, too stunned to reply.

Later that week (after a phone call from Alice), Roberta calls an emergency prayer meeting, and the Christian ladies kneel down on the Bakhtiari carpets in her living room and pray. (I think they are praying for Mansoor. It is only years later I realize they are praying for me.)

God must have heard their prayers. I don't stab Mansoor with a butcher knife like his father picked up so many years ago. But I can't go on like this. Not many days later, I lock myself in the ladies' room at the United Nations, determined not to come out until I have a personal encounter with God.

In desperation, still not knowing how to go about it, I pull a ragged tract out of my purse that I had tossed there months ago. *Ask Jesus to take over your life.* I have nothing to lose so I comply.

Ask forgiveness for your sins. Sins? I have never cheated, robbed, or lied. I don't consider myself a sinner, but just to get it over with, I mumble, "Please forgive me."

That's it. I unlock the door and leave the ladies' room in a strangely peaceful frame of mind.

I never report this ladies' room encounter to Roberta, but she must have guessed. She now treats me more like a believer and less like a seeker.

Much later, I read the parable in which Jesus likens the kingdom of God to a mustard seed, the size of a speck, that slowly grows into a tree. In just that way, something is growing, ever-so-slowly, inside of me.

Now that I am a follower of Jesus Christ, what do I believe? I still have unanswered questions, so I read everything I can get my hands on. An American couple live only a few blocks away, and they allow me to use their library. I start at the top shelves and work my way down. I fall in love with C.S. Lewis' *The Screwtape Letters*, the *Narnia* series and his outer space trilogy.

The biography of Hudson Taylor, founder of the Inland China Mission, leaves me cold. How could he live with himself after burying three wives and numerous children in the bleak soil of China?

The story of the intrepid British missionary, Henry Martyn, is more acceptable to me. He died burning up with fever, in the sands of the Caspian region. At least he had the sense to remain single.

One day in the office, Marina hands me a thick paperback book. "Read this. You'll love it."

"Who is the author?" I ask. Not that it matters, I will read anything.

Marina tosses her long, honey-colored hair back and replies, "Edgar Cayce, the nineteenth century psychic."

Marina is well educated and speaks Russian, Greek, Armenian, French, and English. She even worked as a translator for the UN headquarters in New York. Her beauty and intellect impress me.

"Thanks," I say taking the book. I read it from start to finish in one evening and find Cayce has answers to all the questions troubling a new believer like myself. He explains why good people suffer sickness, disease, and accidents. He has an answer for everything.

Thrilled with this newfound knowledge, I rush over to visit my friends, Shan and Dick Dryer. I burst into their apartment expecting them to be as excited as I am with the Cayce book. Instead, they pause and look at each other with such gravity that I know I have said something wrong.

"The Bible simply does not confirm Edgar Cayce's ideas," Dick finally says.

"Christians don't have all the answers. Beware of anyone who claims to," Shan adds.

I feel deflated, but instinctively know they're right. The way of faith is not cut and dried. It's fraught with ambiguities and uncertainties.

Some months later, Dick suggests a meeting between Reza, a Christian convert from Islam, and Mansoor and his Uncle Nosrollah, the Muslim scholar. Not really a debate, just a friendly sharing of ideas, he says.

I hesitate to set up the meeting because it was Dick who gave his Christian testimony at our first Thanksgiving dinner in Teheran. Mansoor still has a grudge against him. To my surprise, Mansoor is keen on the idea of a theological debate. *Mohammed versus Jesus.* Nothing has so captured his imagination in years.

Dick and Reza arrive at the appointed time. Reza appears nervous and uses the bathroom several times. Uncle Nosrollah, like a senior statesman, is polite and gracious.

I intend to stay in the kitchen for several reasons. One, the level of Farsi spoken will be over my head. Second, someone needs to keep the debaters supplied with glasses of hot tea, fruit, and nuts. This is to be a formal, civilized discussion, and it will proceed slowly and methodically.

I serve the opening round of tea and retreat to the kitchen doorway. Uncle Nosrollah nods to the younger man to begin his defense of Christianity. Reza's face is stiff with tension as he defers, politely insisting that the older man open the debate.

Uncle Nosrollah is unfailingly polite, though converts to Christianity are despised in the Muslim culture. Some families will go so far as to kill a son or daughter who converts. This despite the fact that Islam is a religion of peace. The primary meaning of the word *islam* is peace and, secondarily, surrender.

Uncle begins, and I recognize at once that he is not giving the same speech he gave to me some months ago on the minutiae of daily religious observances for women: the washing of hands and feet, the ceremonial cleansing of dishes and cookware, or why a menstruating woman should refrain from prayers. Rather, he starts with an explanation of the Five Pillars of Islam. Listening through the open kitchen door as I arrange cookies on a plate, I strain to understand his words.

"You have known the straight path from your early childhood." Uncle looks at Reza. He is speaking in the rhythmic, melodic cadence that is intoned in the mosque.

I'm aware that this style of speaking is capable of stirring emotions to the highest pitch. I've read portions of the Koran in an English translation and it seems banal, even convoluted. When spoken aloud, as Uncle is now doing, it sounds like sheer poetry.

Reza looks wary and somehow guilty as Uncle continues.

"God revealed the truth of monotheism through Abraham. Second, God revealed the Ten Commandments through Moses. Third, God revealed the Golden Rule through Jesus. This was not enough. God revealed to Mohammed the Five Pillars of Islam, the principles that regulate the private life of Muslims in their dealings with God."

"Yes, yes, I was taught the first pillar before I was five years old. *There is no god but Allah, and Mohammed is His Prophet.*" Reza quotes the creed in a subdued tone.

"Then you know the second pillar adjures the faithful to be constant in prayer. Five times a day you must praise God: on arising, when the sun reaches its zenith, its mid-decline, sunset, and before retiring."

Reza makes no reply.

"The third pillar of Islam is charity. Two and one half percent of all you own must be given to those less fortunate."

I know Uncle Nosrollah is raising three orphans in his home, along with his natural children. He practices what he preaches. I also know that after Reza became a Christian, he prepared a lavish dinner party and invited the garbage collector, the street cleaners, and the servants in response to Jesus' admonition to entertain those who cannot repay you in kind.

"The fourth pillar of Islam, the observance of Ramadan, is Islam's holy month. During it, Mohammed received his initial revelation, and ten years later he made his historic migration from Mecca to Medina. To commemorate these two great occasions, we Muslims fast for one month. From the first moment of dawn to the setting of the sun, neither food nor drink nor smoke passes our lips. After sundown we may partake in moderation."

Big deal. They eat a major feast when the sun goes down and then a hearty breakfast before sunup, I'm thinking to myself.

Uncle Nosrollah continues, "The fifth pillar is pilgrimage or *haj*. Once during his or her lifetime every Muslim who is physically and economically in a position to do so is expected to journey to Mecca."

"Upon reaching Mecca, pilgrims remove their normal attire, which carries marks of social status, and don two simple sheet-like garments. Everyone is equal before God," Reza replies.

My eyes dart back and forth between Reza and Uncle. Is Reza capitulating so early in the debate?

Uncle briefly touches on the subjects that he had earlier discussed with me in our private discussion. "As you well know, Muslims should not gamble, steal, lie, eat pork, drink alcohol, or be sexually promiscuous."

Reza's face is blank. I can only guess at his response. I hope he isn't impressed with Uncle's reiteration of Muslim dogma anymore than I am.

"God created the world, and after it, human beings. The first man was Adam," Uncle Nosrollah says in his melodious voice.

I pause with my tray of tea balanced in both hands. Did he say Adam? Like in the Biblical account?

"Then Abraham passed the supreme test when he was willing to sacrifice his son Ishmael. The name *Islam* was provided in this extreme act of surrender."

Wait a minute. This doesn't sound right. The Bible says Abraham offers up Isaac, *the son of promise*, not Ishmael, *the son of the bond woman*. I'm beginning to realize there is a big difference between the Bible's version and the Koran's version of the same event. But I say nothing.

Uncle continues, "Abraham had two sons, the first with Hagar and the second with Sarah. According to the Koran, Ishmael went to the place where Mecca was to rise. His descendants, flourishing in Arabia, became Muslims; whereas those of Isaac, who remained in Palestine, were Hebrews and became Jews."

"Yes, the Jews are the *People of the Book*. So are Christians." Reza's voice raises a notch.

Uncle ignores the younger man and calmly continues. "The Jews are correct in their creed: *Hear O Israel, the Lord our God, the Lord is One*. The Christians compromised their monotheism by deifying Christ. Nevertheless, Islam honors Jesus as a prophet and accepts his virgin birth. According to the Koran, Adam's and Jesus' souls are the only two that God created directly."

I silently serve the tea, then stand in the open kitchen door to hear the rest.

"I can't emphasize this strongly enough. The Koran draws the line at the doctrine of the Incarnation and the Trinity." Uncle speaks in a tone of righteous indignation.

Dick starts to protest, but Reza raises his eyebrows a fraction of an inch, as if to say *let him continue.*

"It is not proper for God to have children. Monotheism is Islam's contribution not only to the Arabs, but to the world. To say that God has begotten a son is a grievous thing. Allah has no consort and therefore no heir. There is no son of God."

Uncle is now shouting in his vehemence, and I fear he will wake the children. I narrow my eyes and look at Mansoor, who shrugs and ignores my concern. I make a quick exit to see if the boys are awake. I find them sleeping soundly and kiss their foreheads lightly. When I return to the living room, Reza is speaking. I've missed something important, no doubt.

He pauses to gulp down the last of his tea, then begins in a level tone of voice. "Jesus Christ, Son of God, Savior. What do these words mean?"

I expect him to answer the question of Christ's paternity, but I am wrong.

"The Atonement, Jesus' voluntary death on the cross, for no doubt he could have eluded the Roman soldiers if he had wanted to, is the center of Christianity. Sin came into the world through Adam's disobedience. Infinite sin demands infinite recompense. It required death. God made this payment through the assumption of guilt by his Son and the debt is canceled." Reza stares at his hands then looks Uncle directly in the face. "Those are just words, doctrine. What does this mean to me in actual experience?"

I can tell this is a rhetorical question. He expects no answer from Mansoor or Uncle.

"Love. I have been overtaken by love. In the words of Saint Paul, *the love of Christ constrains me.* Or put another way, love is not just one of God's attributes but instead is God's very essence."

Uncle looks calmly at Mansoor and splits open a pistachio. It is obvious to me that neither is moved by Reza's words.

"As a Muslim scholar, I can not affirm your idolatrous belief in three separate gods. Even the Jews choke on your insistence of the Triune God. You cannot truly be a monotheist," Uncle responds.

Dick stands up and speaks, using wide hand gestures. "Doesn't water assume states that are liquid, solid, and gaseous while retaining its chemical identity? So too does God retain His original identity while appearing in the form of Jesus and the Holy Spirit. Three in one. It's so beautifully simple." Dick smiles at everyone in the room. I can see that he is perfectly at ease as he continues. "Jesus said, *the Father will give you another Counselor, to be with you forever, even the Spirit of truth.*"

Mansoor looks nonplused. He turns to his Uncle whose countenance is inscrutable. Then he looks in my direction. "Shareen, more tea."

I go back to the kitchen to make more tea. A Persian housewife would already have a second pot of strong, black tea simmering on the samovar. I have to start from scratch. First I boil the water. Then I empty the teapot of the sodden tea leaves, put in five teaspoons of fragrant Darjeeling tea and pour in the boiling water. While the brew steeps, I refill the sugar bowl with lumps of hard sugar. After five minutes, I pour the dark liquid in the little glasses. It looks too strong so I dilute the tea with boiling water.

I serve the third and mutually understood last round of tea. We all know the debate is essentially over. There is another twenty minutes of polite talk, "*you are always welcome in my home, I am your servant . . .*"

After finishing their tea, the four men stand and shake hands. I come out of the kitchen to say goodnight to Reza and Dick. As soon as they're out the front door, I turn to see Mansoor patting his Uncle on the shoulder. He is giddy with excitement.

"We certainly showed them," Mansoor chortles.

"Yes, we did," replies the smiling Uncle Nosrollah.

Knowing the debate went their way depresses me as I clear the table of orange peels, pistachio shells, and empty glasses. I had high hopes that Mansoor might one day convert to Christianity. After all, Reza is married to an English woman who attends the same Bible study that I do. If it could happen to her husband, why not mine?

Now, seeing Mansoor and his Uncle jumping up and down with excitement, I no longer cherish that illusion. Later, I learn that the debate is a pivotal turning point in Reza's walk of faith. He went into the discussion unsure of himself and the claims of the Bible. He thought a respected Muslim scholar would tear his defense to shreds. The exact opposite happened. Uncle Nosrollah's defense of Islam sounded hollow in Reza's ears. All the rules and prohibitions of Islamic law paled in comparison to his own faith in a living savior. In fact, as soon as Reza and Dick stood on the sidewalk in front of our house, they jumped up and down with joy and victory.

Despite my unhappy home life, I find Teheran is not such a bad place to live. I have a good job with friendly colleagues. I have two beautiful sons, who are healthy and happy despite the discord in our home. Everyday, when I get home from work, we take a siesta as all work stops and shops close between two and four. Then the boys and I go out for social visits. We don't own a car, but taxis are cheap, as are all luxuries such as hairdressers, maids, or cut flowers. On the other hand, necessities such as food, clothing, and housing are expensive.

Iranians have a rich social fabric. Visits must be made when someone gets engaged, married, has a new baby, travels abroad, or returns from abroad. There are any number of reasons to show up at a friend's house with your arms full of flowers or cake.

I try to celebrate every holiday, both Persian and Christian. The Persian new year, celebrated at the beginning of spring, is especially fun. Everybody gets new clothes, and there is a frenzy of visiting, starting at the home of the eldest member of the family and continuing through everyone down to the youngest. All this coming and going of relatives distracts me from the lovelessness of my marriage.

On Christmas, I get the biggest tree possible, then I invite to the house as many people as possible because I know Mansoor will behave civilly when company is present. The more unhappy I am, the more I throw myself into entertaining.

Shadwin is two years old and still doesn't have a birth certificate or passport. Without telling Mansoor, I return to the hospital where he was born and get a letter from the doctor. Next, I must go to the American consulate and register his birth. I know the consulate is not far from the American Embassy, but I have never been there.

With Shadwin in tow, I walk down what I think is the correct street and enter a large, five-story building on the corner. I don't see the American flag, but this is only a consulate, not the Embassy.

All the windows are painted gray, so no one can see in or out. In the lobby, a man in a business suit comes out of an office and asks me what I want.

"I've come for a birth certificate."

The man mumbles what I think is, "Follow me." Hand in hand with Shadwin, I follow him into a nearby office. Abruptly, he stops and shouts, "I said go no farther!"

I stand there frozen with shock. Government officials don't speak like this. I'm confused and scared. I instinctively pick Shadwin up and hold him in my arms.

Another man, dressed in an identical black suit, enters the room. "What do you want here?" he demands.

"Isn't this the American consulate?" My voice squeaks with fear.

"No Madame, this is not the U.S. Consulate. One street over." He stiffly escorts us out.

At the entrance to the U.S. Consulate, I learn from the Iranian doorman (only embassies have U.S. Marine guards) that I had stumbled into the headquarters of SAVAK, the Shah's secret police.

I'm trying to nap through the heat of the day. Both boys are passed out on their beds. A fan stirs the heavy air in the room. Mansoor is in the hall talking on the telephone. I hear his voice but can't make out the words. I doze off.

Muffled sobs penetrate my consciousness. Am I crying in my sleep? Is it the children? I sit up, curious but not alarmed. I pad softly in to the boys' bedroom. Rodwin is snoring gently. Shadwin sleeps with his thumb in his mouth. The muffled sounds continue through the thick brick walls of the family compound.

I slip out into the hall. The sobbing comes from the back of the house. I walk barefoot down the long hall to the kitchen. It's empty. The sounds come from behind the pantry door. Cautiously, I pull the door open.

Mansoor is standing in the farthest corner, his hands over his mouth, trying to stifle the sobs that wrack his body.

"Are you hurt? What is it?" I ask in alarm.

"Mama Badri is dead!" He moans in unfeigned anguish.

Now I know that he was talking on the telephone to his younger sister who lives in Sweden. Three months previously, she had sent Mama Badri a ticket to Stockholm for a stomach operation.

I put my arms around Mansoor's shoulders as I would to comfort my children. He stiffens and turns away, refusing to let me console him. The years of strife stand between us like a brick wall.

I cry for him. I cry for the loss of my mother-in-law. She had always been kind to me. I cry even harder because of the sad state of my marriage.

Mama Badri's body is shipped from Sweden to Iran the next morning. Like the rest of the family, I don black apparel, black shoes, black stockings, no jewelry. I will dress like this for seven days.

Her elderly sisters receive her body at the mortuary. They open the coffin, remove her clothing, and wash her remains in accordance with Muslim requirements. They wring their hands and cry when they see the long red scar running down her abdomen. Gently, with loving tenderness, they wash their dead sister from head to foot, then wrap her in white linen.

I'm strangely comforted when I learn these details from Pari, Mansoor's older sister. Who better to touch Mama Badri after death than her own kin? I think this arrangement is better than the American way of paying strangers to prepare the deceased.

There is no embalming practice in Islam, so a person is buried as quickly as possible after death. Mama Badri died on the operating table in Stockholm, so her remains were embalmed. Nevertheless, the burial proceeds immediately. The fine Swedish coffin is discarded, as Muslims use only a cloth shroud. A thick Persian carpet enfolds her during transportation to the cemetery. At the open grave, Mama Badri is gently rolled out of the carpet to her final earthly resting place.

Only the male relatives attend the actual burial, but seven days later, I will go with the family to a special graveside ceremony. In the meantime, a memorial service is scheduled at the local mosque.

I carefully get ready, wearing my best black dress. Then I cover myself in a chador made of thick black lace. I've never been in a mosque before, so I imitate every move of my sister-in-law, Pari. When she covers her face, I do the same. When she bows with her head to the floor, I follow suit. When she stands with arms upraised, I raise my arms.

It's a large, modern mosque. Windows in the domed ceiling fill the sanctuary with light. The men are seated on one side and the women on the other behind a partition. A mullah recites from the Koran. The men chant in response. The mosque is filled with relatives and friends. Mama Badri would be pleased.

I recall the dream she related to the family shortly before her trip to Sweden. She was in a lush, green garden beside a river. Her throat was parched and dry. A man, dressed in white cotton trousers and a dazzling white turban, stood by the river with a small basket on a pole.

"Come drink living waters," he said to Mama Badri.

I believe that she is in heaven with God and all the angels. I know she was a practicing Muslim, and Christian theologians might disagree with me. I only know what I feel in my heart.

I look up into the balcony above the women's section and see several of my friends from the Bible study. Their heads are covered in accordance with local custom. They've come to support me. They've also come out of respect for Mama Badri. I've told them what a kind woman she was, a faithful wife and mother, never gossiping or criticizing anyone.

Afterward, the immediate family and close friends go back to Pari's home for a meal. We sit on the floor around a spotless white tablecloth covered with dishes of meat and rice, salads and vegetables. In deliberate contrast to the somber events of the morning, the talk is animated and lively.

Mansoor's best friend and his German wife elect not to come to the meal. Later, Barbara tells me how depressed she and her husband were all the rest of that day. If only they had come to eat with us. Food and companionship are necessary to revive the spirits of the living.

On the seventh day after the burial, the family returns to the cemetery for the *Haft*, or seventh day ceremony. According to Muslim tradition, the soul of the deceased hovers above the grave for seven days, then departs. On this day, the family comes for a farewell feast.

Mansoor and I drive south in a borrowed car and soon leave the crowded city streets behind. An oil refinery pollutes the air. Then we're in true desert, but the air is still thick, burning my throat. There are no trees, and the road dips into valleys and climbs small ranges. From a small hilltop, I see a salt lake that surprises me.

"What's that called?"

He laughs in a way that reveals his deep bitterness toward all the political powers of his country. "SAVAK dumps bodies there. They toss them out of helicopters, some dead, some still alive."

I shiver, though the heat is now intense. To the left of the lake I see a cemetery. We park the car and carefully walk among the gravestones. Mansoor's sister and his nieces and nephews have arrived before us. They have placed a white cloth on the burial mound, then arranged mountains of little cakes, cookies, candies, and fruit. I watch this tableau unfold with mounting unease.

"I can't possibly eat here," I whisper to Mansoor. The thought of eating off Mama Badri's grave makes me sick.

"You're not supposed to. Wait and see." He turns his head to look at the crowd of men, women, and children approaching us.

"Where have all these beggars come from?" I recognize that they are beggars by their tattered, dirty clothing and unkempt hair.

"They live here at the cemetery."

"This is how they get their food?" My voice betrays my horror. Living in the middle-class neighborhood of northern Teheran has shielded me from the reality of the stark poverty that exists in Iran. I have never seen such need.

A hand with ragged dirty fingernails touches my sleeve. I shudder involuntarily. Another hand reaches between us and snatches an orange off the grave. Desperation is causing the beggars to take what they can, now, before the ceremony is over. The crowd behind us is pushing and shoving. In a few minutes it will be a free-for-all.

Mansoor grabs my arm and pulls me away from the grave. "We're leaving! Now!"

He gets no argument from me. We turn and run through the milling strangers. In the parking lot, we get in the car. He locks the doors and starts the engine. I'm relieved that we left Rodwin and Shadwin home with the servant.

"What about your sister and the others?" I'm appalled to think that we're leaving them behind.

"They know how to take care of themselves. Besides, they came in their own vehicles."

In the distant background, the Teheran refinery belches smoke and flames in the air, giving the scene a hellish cast. The lake looks greenish in the middle, the edges fringed with white, cake-like salt. We drive without speaking through the dreary, barren desert back to Teheran. I'm painfully aware that, with Mama Badri's death, something good and noble has ceased to exist in the family.

The sweltering heat and dust of the Teheran summer passes, and icy blizzards cover the streets and flat-roofed buildings with snow. It's winter, and Mansoor sets up a kerosene heater in the largest room in the house. We and the children eat and sleep in this one warm room. The rest of the house stays closed off until spring.

By now I have read all the material I can get my hands on about the Holy Spirit. Then I hear about a couple passing through Teheran on their way to India who have a ministry of laying on of hands.

I'm willing to try anything, so I knock on their hotel room door and introduce myself.

"I want to receive the Holy Ghost."

They look nonplussed, or maybe they are just tired. They tell me to kneel by the bed. Then they put their hands on my head and pray.

They pray and pray and I weep copious tears, but with no results. Embarrassed to be their first failure, I stand up, blow my nose, thank them, and leave the hotel.

The skies are lead gray, the house cold enough to hang beef, and Mansoor speaks to me with curses and words of contempt. To lighten the atmosphere for the boys, I suggest we buy a yellow canary. Mansoor vetoes that idea.

"Birds are unlucky," he says curtly.

I sense something new in the house, a palpable presence of evil. Now I never let Mansoor see me reading my Bible. I hide it before he comes home, but he discovers it each time. I sadly come to the conclusion that God does not exist after all. His opposite, *Shaitan*, as the devil is called in Farsi, seems alive and well.

This depressing shift in my theological position presents a problem. How can I continue to go to the Bible study? I will have to tell my friends that I no longer believe in the existence of God, Jesus, or the Holy Spirit. I never understood the concept of the trinity anyway.

Determined to make a clean break, I go for the last time for tea and scriptures. I intend to tell Roberta my new situation after everyone leaves. The Bible study proceeds as usual. During the final few minutes, Jimi Old, a beautiful silver-haired woman whose husband works for the oil consortium, asks if she can pray for me. I'm embarrassed to say no, so I quietly submit, hoping she will get it over with quickly. Jimi prays intensely and I feel like a hypocrite.

"Stop praying! I don't believe anymore." My tongue feels thick like it is frozen. "Quit praying for me." Now I can't control my tongue. I'm speaking gibberish without my volition. I look up at my friends. Why are they laughing? Why do they have tears in their eyes?

Once again, I try to tell them I don't believe in God, but I can't control my tongue. *What the hell's going on?* Then I understand their laughter. I am speaking in tongues, the unknown language of angels.

The realization that God has touched me with His Holy Spirit at the same time that I am denying His existence shatters my composure and I begin to weep.

After this event, I never again doubt the existence of God or his love for me. Yet, I do not become a saint, and Mansoor does not become more civil. Still, I have something tangible to hold on to. My heart is fixed, to quote the psalmist, and I can't turn back.

Two

My first visit to a church is prompted by a tragedy experienced by my friends Roberta and Jim. Death visited their little family compound on an ordinary summer day, when seven-year-old David climbed on top of his garden wall and seized a live power line to steady himself. Roberta glanced out the living room window and saw him fall. She screamed in disbelief as his lifeless body hit the ground.

Jim was in London on business when he received the telegram telling him of his son's death. On the plane back to Iran, he looked out the window and composed a poem that was read at the memorial service and later printed in the English language Teheran *Journal*.

David, David where are you,
exploring some place new?
Where is the son I left last week,
outside playing hide and seek.

Where did you get to, David *jan*,
out someplace beyond the dawn?
Beyond the morning star,
far beyond what we call far.

Daddy, last night something made
me very, very much afraid.
I climbed up on the wall to play.
I don't know just what to say.

Happened there, something hot,
I touched - it hurt an awful lot.
I cried and cried, and then I ran,
I ran until I saw this man.

And daddy, guess who it could be?
Jesus, and He remembered me.
He said, David have no fears.
I know what to do with tears.

And then He took me right away,
straight to God the shortest way.
Right up through this way of light,
God picked me up and held me tight.

And wiped the tears right off my face,
and said, no tears are in this place.
I am your Father, David boy,
You see that here, we just have joy.

The memorial service is held at the Community Church in Teheran, a charming old stone building surrounded by a lush rose garden. After the service, Roberta and Jim give candy to David's friends and classmates as a way to celebrate David's life.

I'm still stunned by the accident and at the same time, I feel a sense of awe as I observe how Roberta and Jim react to the death of their son. They know something about eternity that I don't know. I feel like someone on the outside looking in. A believer in God, yet still a bystander. I gaze at a sky that resembles a turquoise bowl turned upside down. I realize there is more to this business of faith than is readily apparent to a new believer like me.

A few months later, a missionary family, traveling at night with their children, plows into a parked truck on the side of the road. All the children die. Once again, I attend a memorial service in the lovely old stone chapel. I'm deeply shaken as I listen to the bereaved father play his trumpet. What strength enables him to do so?

This is so different from the Muslim way of facing death. Mama Badri's funeral is still fresh in my mind. Then there was Mansoor's teenage cousin, who fell off the roof and died. His family sat on the floor of their living room for seven days and wept without restraint. They still wear black clothing and will do so until the first anniversary of his death.

Outside the church, I overhear some Iranians talking after the funeral. They have come to the conclusion that Christians must not love their children. I know differently, but I can't explain it.

My marriage problems seem small compared to the loss of these young children, but I reach the point where I can't continue. One morning, after washing my face at the sink, I look at myself in the mirror. For the first time in years, I really look at myself. Not the quick glance as I brush my unruly hair back and dab on lipstick. This time I stare into my hazel eyes and see a defeated woman. What I see makes me cringe. Why do I let it go on year after year? From somewhere, deep inside, a spirit of resolve enters my being, causing me to stand straighter. I have made a decision. Come what may, I will no longer tolerate Mansoor's verbal abuse. I will no longer pretend to be deaf when he calls me a *sonofabitch American* in front of my children. I bide my time and wait for him to come home that afternoon. I feel powerful. This is not the cringing, acquiescent Shareen that Mansoor is used to. I will unleash on his unsuspecting head every curse I've ever heard him use.

Your father is a dog and may he burn in hell. I'm just getting warmed up. *You're a camel's arsehole, a brother of a homosexual pig.* I find I am unexpectedly fluent in Farsi. *Bastard spawn of corpse-eating vultures. Murdering rapist of your own grandmother.*

His eyes burn like coal in his pale face. I pause for breath, but before I can unleash another volley of insults, he grabs me by both arms, drags me through the house, out the garden, and shoves me into the alley. Furious, I run back inside. He drags me out again. Again I run back. Shadwin starts bawling, and I stop to console him. How can two adults behave like this in front of a child? I'm grateful Rodwin is at school and is spared this ugly scene.

"We can't do this in front of Shadi. I'll leave quietly," I say at last. I know the marriage is irrevocably over. I have committed the unforgivable. And I'm proud of myself. I pick up my purse and walk out the door with my head held high. I don't break down until I'm out of sight and hearing. That day, I arrange to move in with Jim's sister, Ginger.

Ginger's name fits her perfectly. Her long auburn hair flows in waves to her waist. She shares an apartment with Ruthann, who possesses equally beautiful but blonde hair. They both part their hair in the middle and wear little or no makeup in the style of the 1960s.

Ginger came to Teheran to visit her brother, loved the city, and stayed. Ruthann came to visit her Iranian roommate from university days and stayed for the same reason.

They sense my despair and vow between themselves never to leave me alone. Their fear that I will commit suicide is not unfounded. Every night, as soon as the lights go out, I lie on the pallet in the sitting room and silently cry.

In time, a gradual change begins, at least in my outward demeanor. I quit teasing and spraying my hair into a French twist, and trade my dresses and high heels for skirts or jeans. Instead of emulating sophisticated Teheran women, I feel more like myself. I'm coming to terms with the separation and even hope for the day that I will have custody of my sons. I'm aware of the Muslim law that gives the father custody of boys (a daughter may stay with her mother until the age of six). But I know from past experience that Mansoor will not be able to support himself. Therefore, I suspect he will reluctantly give me custody at some point down the road. I'm prepared to wait it out.

Thinking I need a diversion, Ruthann and Ginger invite me on a train journey, southward across the barren wastelands, to the city of Shiraz. I gratefully accept.

Knowing that the people outside of Teheran are more religious, we dress modestly in long-sleeved cotton dresses, worn over trousers. We cover our hair with scarves. At the inn in Shiraz, we change into evening gowns and hire a taxi to take us to Persepolis to attend a concert by Ravi Shankar, the Indian sitar player. For one magical night, the towering pillars and crumbling palaces of ancient Persia regain past glory. The *Shahbanu*, Empress Farah, is present with most of her court. Hyenas and jackals, howling under the full yellow moon, accompany the high, thin twang of the sitar. In this strange setting, I live my dream of being a princess, at least for one night.

Some weeks later, Ruthann and I visit the city of Mashad, famous for its gold-covered mosque and the tomb of the Eighth Imam. We ride the train five hundred miles north to where Iran meets with the border of Russia and Afghanistan. Ruthann knows about a hostel used by American hippies traveling overland to Kabul. We check in and right away I notice the absence of a lock on our door.

"Wouldn't we be safer in a real hotel?" I ask.

"We'd have to fend off advances from men in an expensive hotel. Trust me," she replies.

The hippies are friendly and, more importantly, don't put any moves on us. They even tell us where to eat a good, cheap lunch.

Motivated by a spirit of curiosity mixed with chutzpah, I ask our innkeeper's wife to lend me a chador and take me inside the famous mosque. I know it is forbidden to foreigners, just like Mecca is off limits to non-Muslims. But I figure that I am entitled to blur the edges of reality a bit here. After all, I do have an Iranian passport.

"Not possible," she says, recognizing I'm a foreigner by my heavily accented Farsi.

"My sons are *Seyyed*," I tell her. Of course she knows this is a hereditary title passed down from father to son beginning with Ali, the husband of Mohammed's daughter, Fatimah. Seyyeds are held in highest esteem in the Shi'ite world.

"My Muslim name is Fatimah," I add in case she need even more incentive.

As I anticipated, she is swayed by my degree of closeness to the House of Ali. This is the first and last time I ever trade on that distinction.

Although reluctant, she loans me a plain black chador. "Pull it over your forehead and around your face so only your eyes show," she commands me.

She takes my hand and we leave the inn and join a crowd of pilgrims in the street. A faint roar in the distance sounds like a mountain waterfall. The closer we get to the mosque the louder the noise becomes. When I realize the sound is a great crowd of men shouting in unison, I hesitate to go farther. The innkeeper's wife tugs me forward.

In the outer courtyard of the mosque, dozens of men are beating their bare chests with wooden clubs, the dull thud resounding off bare flesh and bone in counterpoint to their chant *Allah akbar*, God is great. I remember, belatedly, that foreigners make a point of staying indoors during the self-flagellation performed during *Moharram*, a passion play reenacting the death of Imam Hussein. My mouth is dry, my knees tremble, and I want to turn back.

Veiled from head to foot, the innkeeper's wife walks briskly past the men without looking at them. I have no choice but to continue with her through another door. In contrast to the scene in the courtyard, the inside of the mosque resembles a magical fairyland. I try to erase the disturbing scene of men beating themselves as I gaze at gigantic crystal chandeliers bouncing light off millions of tiny mirror mosaics. Before I have time to appreciate the aesthetics of the mosaics, my companion pulls me into the inner chamber. The rather small and plain tomb of the Eighth Imam is protected by iron grillwork.

A crowd of men and women surge in concentric circles around the tomb, moving closer and closer with each round. Waves of frenzied emotion emanate from the pilgrims as they stretch out their hands to caress the metal grating. Some tie bits of cloth to it as symbols of their petitions. Women are moaning in ecstasy. Men are hoarse with heartfelt prayer.

More and more people enter the chamber. The press of bodies carries us closer and closer to the tomb. Religious frenzy is consuming everyone. Except me. With belated clarity, I know I do not belong here. A spiritual voice, alien to anything I have ever known, whispers, “You will be torn to pieces if they find out you’re not a Muslim.”

With my eyes, I mutely convey my desperation to leave. The innkeeper’s wife skillfully maneuvers us through the crowd until we find ourselves on the sidewalk. We walk back to the inn without talking.

The next morning, Ruthann and I take the train back to Teheran. During the long journey I have time to reflect on my foolhardiness of the day before.

“I had no right to visit that mosque,” I say to Ruthann. I try but fail to explain the weird sense of an alien presence in the mosque. The spooky voice that warned me to get out of the inner chamber did me a favor. Why do I feel goosebumps when I think about it?

"I agree," she replies succinctly. Ruthann is a chemistry major and is, as ever, pragmatic and sensible in her outlook on life.

I gaze out the window at a camel caravan on the horizon. I'm grateful to be heading back to Teheran. I vow I will never again set foot in a mosque.

One afternoon, as I walk to the market, a police jeep pulls alongside the curb. I glance at the driver and keep walking. I don't know who he wants, but it isn't me. He couldn't have been waiting outside the apartment building. Or could he? I know that the police have no authority to enter and arrest someone in their home. I also know that the judicial system in Iran holds that a person is guilty until he can prove his own innocence. But what have I done? Nothing. I keep walking, eyes straight ahead. The jeep keeps pace. I hesitate at the intersection.

"Get in," the policeman commands. The option of running is out. Where would I run? And why? Bewildered, I comply. We drive to a small police station near the United Nations office building. I'm in a familiar neighborhood and don't feel alarmed. It must be a case of mistaken identity. I ask the officer in charge why I have been picked up. He shrugs and gives me no answer. I sit in front of his desk for over an hour. Evidently, the police don't know why I am there and what to do with me.

Then I overhear a whispered conversation about "her husband." Now I understand. Mansoor is behind this. I pick up the phone on the desk and dial my sister-in-law's home. Panic is building in the back of my mind, however much I keep telling myself not to worry.

"Pari, it's Shareen. I'm being held at the police station." I try to control the sharp edge of hysteria in my voice.

"I can do nothing," she replies and hangs up.

Now I'm frightened. I call my friend Roberta. While I'm explaining what happened and where they're holding me, the sergeant snatches the phone out of my hand.

"You think this is a party?" He slams the phone back on the desk. With no further explanation he orders me back into the jeep.

"Where are you taking me?" I ask the driver.

"To the American Embassy," he replies with a sneer.

I feel tremendous relief, yet something in his voice tells me to stay alert. I wait for him to turn left on the Boulevard where the Embassy is located. My heart sinks when he turns right and heads south to a part of Teheran where I have never been before. Tears well up in my eyes when I realize he has lied to me.

We weave in and out of traffic. The streets are narrow and in need of repair. The jeep hits a pothole that jars me to the bone. The houses and buildings are small and packed together in no discernible architectural pattern. There are no trees or parks. Unlike north Teheran, all the women are in chadors. My ex-housekeeper, Khadije, lives in this part of Teheran. No Americans ever come here.

Soon we leave the impoverished residential area. It looks as if we are now on the outskirts of south Teheran. There is more and more open land, barren and desolate. The police jeep stops in front of a high-walled compound. Behind the wall is a four-story building with small, narrow windows. It's obviously a prison. Crowds of people are standing outside the large metal gate. I assume these are relatives waiting to visit prisoners.

The driver parks the jeep outside the double gate. I get out of the jeep and the policeman directs me to the entrance.

A woman in the crowd calls out, "*Khanoum*, Madame, what did you do?"

I pause, surprised anyone would ask or care. I'm still angry at the way the police lied to me about the American Embassy. I want to hit back, so I reply in a calm voice, "I murdered an Iranian!"

The crowd murmurs audibly, whether in disapproval or approbation I can't tell. Feeling good after this bit of defiance and deception, I step through the small door built in the larger metal gate.

A guard takes me to an office with a desk and two chairs. There, a prison matron comes in and tells me to sit. She has a kind demeanor, but insists I hand over my purse. After searching my handbag, she removes a nail file, then leaves the room. To show that I'm not afraid of what's ahead, I take out a compact and apply lipstick and turquoise blue eye shadow. I will myself not to cry.

The prison matron returns and takes me to an inner courtyard. I'm surrounded on four sides by gray walls. In the middle of one wall is an open storeroom, filled from floor to ceiling with hard, narrow loaves of bread. Will I get only stale bread and water? I think of the freshly baked bread, still warm from the oven, that I usually eat.

I'm not alone. Two women stare at me. One is young, about my age. She wears a chador made of inexpensive material. The other woman has gray hair, partially covered by a scarf. Her flounced skirt over pantaloons tells me she is a village woman. They are both sitting on a wooden bench.

"What did you do, *geigar*, sweetheart?" The older woman sounds sincere.

"I guess I made my husband angry." I take a seat on the end of the bench.

"Then you're in for a long time." She shrugs as if to say, that's that, no need to say more.

Even though I don't ask, she tells me why she is in prison.

"I sell opium. I've lots of friends inside, so I don't mind."

"What about her?" With a lift of my shoulder I indicate the young woman.

"Left her husband in the village. Came to the city to make her way alone. Any woman on the street alone is assumed to be a prostitute."

We sit there all afternoon, apparently forgotten by our jailers. The opium seller, obviously not new to the prison system, explains that the prison cells are full. "They will keep us in this courtyard until space opens up inside."

Inside. The word conjures up frightening memories. One of the ladies in the Bible study had often visited this prison on behalf of the American Embassy. Jimi Old daily brought food to an American woman who was imprisoned for shooting her husband, an oil engineer. During the trial, the woman had claimed self defense, but the eight bullets in her husband's body did not bode well for her. She was given a long sentence.

In prison, she discovered that the guards laced her food with opium. It was common knowledge that once a prisoner is addicted, the guards supplement their meager income by supplying more drugs. So, the American Embassy agreed to provide all her food and asked Mrs. Old to deliver the meals. Mrs. Old heard stories of rapes and beatings.

However, no guard ever succeeded with the American prisoner. She was a tough lady, who didn't hesitate to break a wooden chair over the head of anyone who came too close. According to Mrs. Old, the American prisoner was also a trained nurse. Over time she turned her attentions to the needy women prisoners, as many were pregnant and gave birth alone.

I sat on the hard wooden bench trembling. Jimi Old had shared another story about a Peace Corps girl. The official story in the newspaper was that this girl accidentally died from gas fumes in her hotel room. The American woman in prison told Jimi a different story.

After midnight, when most of the prisoners were asleep, she heard the voice of a young woman, crying and pleading for help. She recognized an American accent. When the first feeble light of daybreak penetrated the prison windows, she saw the matron walk down the corridor with a large hypodermic needle in her hand. Moments later, the moaning and sobbing stopped.

Jimi Old reported this account to an official at the American Embassy. He sadly shook his head. He was powerless to do anything. "We have to accept the official account that this girl asphyxiated due to a faulty heater in her hotel room."

Sitting in this locked courtyard, I dreaded the moment when they would find a cell and transfer me inside. What chance did I have? Could I defend myself by physically intimidating the guards?

To comfort myself, I began to softly sing the one hymn I knew by heart, "How Great Thou Art."

"What are you singing, sweetheart?" asks the opium seller.

"I'm singing about God." Not knowing how to translate the English words into Farsi, I fall silent.

"I didn't know foreigners knew anything about God," the prostitute says to the opium dealer.

Her words humble me. They are women in trouble, just like me. They too look to God.

I sit with my own thoughts until the prison matron returns with the warden. He announces that my mother is making arrangements to get me out. My mother? She isn't in Teheran. Is he playing with my mind? Like the policeman telling me he was taking me to the American Embassy? I don't believe him.

Late that night, the warden releases me into the custody of Jimi and Bob Old. So this is who the warden thought was my mother. I'm so relieved and happy to see them. I say good-bye to the opium dealer and the prostitute. I feel bad because I know they have no one on the outside advocating for their release. They will be here a long time.

In the car, Jimi tells me how they searched for me at the police station near the United Nations building.

"Not one policeman admitted that you had ever been there," Jimi said shaking her head.

"All we had to go on was your call to Roberta," Bob continues. "Getting nowhere with the police, we decided to go directly to the prison."

"The warden and I know each other well," Jimi adds.

"Surely, that wasn't enough to get me out." I had been in Iran too long to underestimate the power of official bureaucracy. "What were the charges against me, anyway?"

"You mean they never told you?" Jimi stared at me, incredulous, while Bob stared straight ahead, his hands gripping the wheel.

"No," I replied.

"Multiple, and I mean multiple, like in a dozen charges of adultery."

"With who?" I blurt, more curious at this point than outraged.

"Let's see. The information officer at the UN. Mansoor had him arrested this morning. He and the UN lawyer have been negotiating with Mansoor all afternoon."

Bob Old tries to lighten the mood in the car. "Then there is the garbage collector, the street sweeper, the baker, and the candlestick maker."

I groan inwardly. How could Mansoor have gotten it so wrong? There had been no adultery with any of the men charged. Still, after moving in with Ruthann and Ginger, I did meet someone at the Iran/American Cultural Center. He works for the CIA, which probably explains why he wasn't picked up and jailed. I certainly did not try to hide my friendship with him.

"How did you persuade Mansoor to drop the charges?"

"Basically, Mansoor has no proof. Still, a husband's accusation is enough for a long imprisonment. The warden didn't seem too eager to have another American woman in his prison. He bent over backward to give Mansoor a chance to withdraw the charges. But

Mansoor was afraid that if he did that, the UN man he accused would sue him for wrongful arrest."

Jimi takes over the rest of the story. "The UN lawyer, you know, Mr. Sarkassian. As an Iranian, he knows how Mansoor's mind works. He offered to give Mansoor a written agreement that states his client will not sue if the charges are dropped."

Bob chuckles so low it sounds like a growl. "At first it was a standoff. *You sign first. No you sign first.* After hours of fruitless negotiations, the lawyer blinked first. It was past 9:00 P.M. He probably wanted to get home. His client signed a statement that he would not sue Mansoor. Then, and only then, did Mansoor sign a paper dropping the charges against you."

"The warden agreed to release you into our custody until an official divorce hearing can be held in the regular courts."

Bob drives smoothly into the underground parking area of his luxurious apartment building. "Welcome to your new home."

I'm not the first person Jimi and Bob Old have rescued. The year before, a young Iranian man from their church had suffered a mental breakdown. He lived with them for six months during his recovery.

Ali had been the caretaker of the American Community Church. He swept the floor, dusted the pews, and lit the kerosene heater before services. After church potlucks and socials, he cleaned up spills and put away the folding tables and chairs. He helped put up the Christmas tree and hid the Easter eggs. After several years he began to relate less and less to his own family and took on an American persona. Sadly, none of the Americans even knew his name.

He felt like an invisible man. His mental state deteriorated. He neglected to shave and change his shirt. The church never got swept or the heater lit before services. Now they noticed him, but it was too late. The board of deacons discussed how to get rid of him with the least amount of termination pay.

Bob Old, the only deacon to protest this policy, suggested that the church pay for his treatment. He was voted down.

Heartsick at the failure of their Christian community to show compassion, Jimi and Bob did what they knew to be right. They paid for the caretaker's psychiatric treatment and took him into their home to live.

"He'll murder you in your bed, you'll see," the deacons warned them.

Even the Iranian psychiatrist thought they had gone too far. "Ali needs to be among his own kind before he will get well."

The young man wept and pleaded with them to let him stay. Neither one had the heart to turn him out. In due course, their generosity and down-to-earth Texan common sense proved the others wrong.

Ali's personality disorder gradually disappeared while he lived like a son of the Old family. He improved so much that he was able to move back with his Iranian family, get a job, and move on with his life.

Now I occupy the guest bedroom and receive their unconditional love and attention. While Bob is at his office at the Iranian Oil Consortium, Jimi and I play tennis at the Officers' Club. This is a new experience for me (Jimi has to lend me white shorts and tennis shoes), as I never before socialized with the large military or expatriate community. This is a side of Teheran life that the Iranians never see. These Americans live as if they are still in the United States. They have their own commissary where they buy American canned goods, cigarettes, and liquor. They have their own country club and church.

Bob Old is required by his position in the oil consortium to participate in this American community. He and Jimi also choose to live and share their lives with the small community of local believers. There is another church in Teheran, the Philadelphia Church, that is led by an Iranian. There is also the Bible study in Roberta's living room, where Iranian women, and those married to Iranians, are not only welcomed but made to feel at home.

I find it easy to adjust to life in this luxurious apartment. It's always easier to adjust up in one's living standards than to adjust downward. Still, I am emotionally conflicted. I visit Rodwin and Shadwin whenever I think Mansoor will not be home. It is not often enough. He has hired a new housekeeper. She tells me she has a year-old baby but someone in her village is raising him so that she can work. My heart aches for her. I know how she feels. Why is life so unfair? I ask myself, knowing there is no answer.

The days pass in uneventful succession as we wait for our day in court. Then my hands break out in a rash.

"I'm sure it's just nerves," Jimi says and sends me to her doctor.

In the waiting room I encounter my CIA friend. My heart beats faster. Has God ordained this? I am breathless as we hug, then sit down in adjoining chairs.

"What are you doing here?"

"I have a rash."

"So do I." We both laugh.

That evening I tell Jimi and Bob about meeting Chris. Silence settles on the dining room table like a blanket. We continue eating, but the conversation is strained.

As I prepare for bed, Jimi comes into my bedroom.

"Shareen, honey." She strokes my long hair falling loose down my back. "Bob wants to have a talk with you before you go to sleep. He's in the living room."

Bob's a big, tall man, real Texan, born in Houston. And the most gentle man I have ever known. He speaks in a soft southern drawl.

"Come sit down, hon. We need to talk." I sit in the chair opposite him.

"This isn't easy for me, y'all understand?"

I nod, but I don't know what I'm agreeing to.

"Shareen, now that you're a Christian and following the Lord, you have to make sacrifices."

I wonder if he means my children.

"It's flat out not acceptable for you to have a lover."

He must mean Chris. I never said he's my lover. Yet the emotional pain I'm feeling right this moment is evidence that he is more to me than a friend. I struggle to control my facial muscles.

Bob doesn't look at me but he senses my distress. "Y'all know, you can't have a husband and a boyfriend at the same time. The Lord won't bless such an arrangement." He gently places his large hand on my knee. "I'm simply reminding you of what you already know."

"Thanks," I murmur. I get up and rush out onto the balcony and sit in a wicker chair. I look at the Teheran sky but I can't see the stars for the tears in my eyes. Despair swallows me up like a black rain cloud bursting without warning. *I have nothing, no one. Am I destined to be a solitary woman without children or husband? Is this what God wants?* I sit on the balcony until after midnight. There is no visitation from a celestial being. No word spoken from heaven. Bob is my guardian angel, and I've just heard from him. I finally go to my bedroom, knowing that he is right. All contact with Chris will cease.

Three

The first court appearance is scheduled for this week. Only Jimi accompanies me because this is just a preliminary hearing. We meet in a small chamber with a Muslim cleric who is in charge of the family court. Jimi and I sit on one side of the room. Mansoor sits on the other. The cleric, dressed in a Western style business suit, reads the papers on his desk, then raises his head and peers at me.

"What do you have to say on your behalf?" he asks, not unkindly.

"My husband is mentally unstable," I reply. I hadn't premeditated what I would say. This just comes out.

Mansoor jumps out of his seat as if he's been bitten by a snake. "Your eminence, she's the one who is crazy!"

The judge looks first at Mansoor, then to me. "Both of you must be examined by a psychiatrist before I make a judgment." He gets up and leaves the room. Mansoor storms out after him. Bewildered, Jimi waits for me to translate what just took place.

The morning of the court-appointed psychiatric examination dawns like every other morning. I drink tea with Jimi on the sunny balcony (Bob has already left for work). The temperature is still pleasant at this time of day.

"Are you sure you want to go alone?" Jimi asks.

I assure her I do. She has done enough for me, and I don't want to wear out my welcome. Of course the deck is stacked against me. It bothers me that Mansoor picked the doctor and booked the appointment. I figure he has already prejudiced the doctor against me. I say none of this to Jimi.

I go by taxi to the doctor's office. I take the elevator to the fourth floor. My heartbeat is racing in anticipation of what I perceive to be an unfair evaluation of my mental state. By the time I enter the office and introduce myself to the secretary I'm in a full blown state of anxiety.

"Go in," she says. "Your husband is already here."

Great, I think, I should have gotten here first. The doctor is seated at his desk. Mansoor is sitting opposite him on his left. I take the chair to his right.

There is minimal fuss over introductions and then the requisite polite formality of shaking hands all around. I sit and self-consciously straighten my skirt. The office is pleasantly furnished with expensive teak furniture, the floor covered with a blue Kashan. Photos of family members are interspersed with book shelves. One photo shows the doctor skiing on Mount Darmavand.

"Tell me, what do you perceive to be the problem here?" The psychiatrist speaks in perfect, American-accented English. He is about my height, which is average for Iranian men. I judge his age to be thirty something. I wonder if he earned his degree at UCLA or USC in Los Angeles, but I am too nervous to ask. I might trust him if he were not a male.

"My husband is incapable of holding a job," I say. I want to establish the state of Mansoor's mental health based on his erratic work history.

"Is that true?" The doctor turns to Mansoor with a mild look on his pleasantly handsome face.

"I have a job." Mansoor reaches in his shirt pocket and takes out a document that implies he is employed. The doctor takes the paper and briefly scans it before handing it back.

It's as if he had anticipated my opening response and had his documentation ready. Of course, the doctor is going to believe him, not me. My level of control is slipping. I've only been here a few minutes and I already feel defeated.

"That paper doesn't mean anything." My voice rises. I take a deep breath.

"Let's leave that issue aside for the moment, shall we?" The doctor's voice is soft and well modulated. "Are you having difficulty sleeping?"

"No," I reply. I don't know where this is leading, but his voice makes me uneasy.

"Do you have a good appetite?"

"I eat plenty, but I'm thin because of the crummy water in Teheran. I've had cholera and dengue fever." My eyes blaze with defiance. "What has any of this have to do with my mental state?"

"Your husband is concerned for you, I assure you."

Yeah, right, I'm thinking. All he wants is my happiness. A taste of bile rises in my throat. This is a waste of time.

Without premeditation, I jump up and bolt out of the doctor's office, startling the secretary as I race by her desk. She runs after me, calling me to come back. Mansoor and the psychiatrist by this time have collected their wits and are right behind her. I reach the elevator and punch the down button. Stepping in, I close the door just in time. My knees are trembling and I'm breathing hard. Now they will think I'm crazy. But I don't care. I just want out of here.

As I approach the exit door, a uniformed policeman steps from the shadows and grabs my wrist.

"You are under arrest."

I can't believe this. Mansoor set this up in advance. It didn't matter how it went with the psychiatrist. I was to be arrested as soon as I came out of the building. Once again, I get into the back seat of a police jeep. The driver, a middle-aged man with a huge mustache, looks at me with sorrowful black eyes.

"How could you do it?" he says.

"What?" I reply. "Do what?"

"Chain your children to their beds and leave them without food."

There is painful silence in the jeep. My heart sinks with despair. How can I defend myself against such lies?

The police jeep maneuvers through the traffic to a familiar neighborhood. Soon we are parked outside Jim and Roberta Dawson's house. We are sitting in the shadow of the very wall where their son David died. Now I understand why the police picked me up. They are going to arrest Jim on Mansoor's orders, and charge him with adultery.

One of the policemen knocks on the door. Roberta answers. They tell her that they are here to pick up her husband. Would he be so kind as to come out so they can arrest him? Roberta goes back in and confers with Jim. Then she comes out to the jeep to talk to me.

"I'm so sorry, Roberta. Please forgive me for bringing this on you and Jim."

"Don't worry. Jim says he's willing to go to prison, if necessary. He thinks maybe he'll get some time to do some writing. But what can I do for you?"

"Bring me a pair of trousers to wear under my short skirt. If I'm going back to prison I want to be adequately covered." Roberta brings me the requested item and Jim accompanies her. "Call Jimi and Bob Old," I shout out the window as the jeep pulls away from the house.

It is a different police station from the first one. But it is as barren and bleak. The walls are painted a drab institutional gray.

The tile floors look like they need a good scrubbing. The policemen act embarrassed to have two Americans under arrest. They take Jim to one room and me to another. I never see him again that night. The room holds one wooden table and two chairs. A bare bulb hangs on a cord from the ceiling.

The officer on duty tries to reason with me. "Please go home with your husband. I assure you, you don't want to go to prison."

That's what he thinks. I would rather go to prison than be under Mansoor's domination again. At least in prison they would have to account for my death.

The day passes somehow. It is now night, and Jimi and Bob Old have been at the station for hours. Everybody is tired, even the policemen. They're trying to convince Mansoor to drop the charges against Jim Dawson. He is charged with committing adultery with me. Mansoor had a detective follow me and saw me enter the Dawson home. Of course, it was a women's Bible study, but what did Mansoor know or care?

After midnight, Mansoor proposes a settlement. If I sign a paper relinquishing my parental rights, then, and only then, will he drop the charges against Jim Dawson. I refuse to sign. What does he need my signature for anyway? As the father, he gets full custody automatically. It is merely more of his psychological warfare.

The strain of the long day and the lateness of the hour is wearing me down. Is this how prisoners of war feel when they are forced to make false confessions? Physical fatigue is breaking down my will to resist. There is no physical torture, but the mental anguish is intense. I'm worried for Roberta and her children. How will she get on with her husband in prison? I'm adamant on one point. I will not let them send me back to Mansoor's house. If I thought he was mentally unstable before, now he is insane. I fear he is capable of locking me up in the cellar for the rest of my life. But how can I sign my name to a document that denies my mother's heart? Again I refuse.

The officer sighs. The blue shadows under his eyes deepen to shades of gray. He leaves me alone for half an hour. I'm cold and my empty stomach growls. I remember the simple breakfast on the patio with Jimi, buttered flat bread with honey. It's been almost twenty-four hours since then. The door opens and an old man in civilian clothes enters with a glass of tea and a bowl of sugar on a tin tray. I gratefully sip the hot, heavily sugared tea. Then Jimi comes in the room and sits down at the table. Fatigue lines the soft, beautiful skin of her face.

"Honey, it's time to wrap this up. Just sign the paper. We need to take you home with us, and Jim can go home also."

"But what about Mansoor? Does he know I will leave with you?" I want to cry but don't.

"Excuse my rough Texan language, but that man doesn't know his ass from a hole in the ground. Bob and the officer on duty have reached an agreement. Just sign it, Shareen."

The ordeal is over for now. (There is still the final court appearance in a few weeks) We all leave the police station. I return to Jimi and Bob's apartment, relieved to be in their good hands. But I'm sad beyond words, a sorrowing that is unspeakable because I know Mansoor will use this worthless piece of paper to prove to Rodwin and Shadwin that I never loved them.

On one level, I won. I am free, and he can't touch me. On a deeper level, he won, and he knows it. The only thing I value is my children. My home, possessions, furnishings, clothing, and jewelry mean nothing to me. I left everything when I walked out of his house. But now he has taken the only thing I treasure.

Mansoor's younger brother also had married an American girl he'd met in college. They lived some years in Sweden. Recently, they've moved to Teheran. Jackie is sympathetic to my situation (unlike the rest of my in-laws) because Mansoor had opposed her marriage to his brother and never lets her forget it. She invites me to a birthday party at her home, assuring me that Rodwin and Shadwin will be there, but Mansoor will not.

I take a taxi to a crowded suburb near Mehrabad Airport. It's a middle-class neighborhood, crowded with apartment buildings. There are no trees or parks like in the more affluent north Teheran. Their apartment is on the ground floor. I knock on the door, my heart trembling. It has been months since I've been together with my boys. Are they as eager to see me as I am to see them?

Jackie opens the door and kisses me on both cheeks Iranian style. I see Rodwin across the living room playing with toys on the tiled floor. His eyes light up when he sees me. He comes over and gives me a big hug. Shadwin watches his brother then bashfully hangs his head. Three months is a lifetime in the mind of a toddler. I'm no longer the primary caregiver, and therefore his affections have centered on his father. It hurts me to see that inscrutable look on little Shadi's face. I have lost something precious and irretrievable.

I go over to him and pick him up. "Hi Shadi." I kiss him tenderly. He wiggles out of my embrace and returns to his games. To hide my pain and uncertainty, I reach in my handbag and take out a pack of cigarettes. I never smoked before, but a secretary at the UN urged me to smoke to calm my nerves. The physical act of striking the match, lighting up, inhaling, and blowing out the flame does more to steady my shaking hands than the nicotine does. I hand Jackie's son, Behzad, his birthday present. He is eight, one year younger than his cousin Rodwin. This is the last family gathering that I will attend.

The day of the final court hearing arrives. Bob Old takes a day off to accompany Jimi and me. We sit on one side of the courtroom. I dress conservatively in a mid-length skirt and a high-necked blouse. My dark hair is pulled back in a ponytail, but I don't wear a head covering like many Iranian women do. Bob is in a blue business suit and Jimi wears a trim dress and jacket with one piece of gold jewelry for accent. The male court recorder, wearing a black suit and a stiffly starched white shirt, sits at a small desk to one side. The windows are open, and street noise disturbs the stillness of the room. It's stifling hot, but no breeze penetrates the bars on the window.

My heart sinks when I see Rodwin sitting next to Mansoor. Why has he brought him into this? A divorce court is no place for a nine-year-old child. The judge reads aloud the charges against me. The words roll off his tongue in great swelling waves. Farsi is a poetic language that rises and falls like the moon pulls and releases the tide. The beauty of his words belie their content—*whore, adulterer, abuser, torturer of children.* There is more, but I mentally disconnect.

The judge removes his glasses and looks in Mansoor's direction. "Do you have anything to add?"

I know I will have no say in these proceedings. It is solely the prerogative of the accuser to speak.

Mansoor leans over and whispers something to Rodwin. He takes him by the elbow and forces him to stand. His arms hang stiffly at his side. I think of the times he would come home from school and recite the poems he learned. Sometimes he would recite in Farsi, sometimes in English. I would try to correct his inflection on certain English words.

"It's pronounced LA-vender, not la-VEN-der."

He would resolutely shake his head. "My teacher says La-VEN-der blue."

I ruefully smile, wondering what Mansoor has forced him to recite for the benefit of the judge.

Mansoor looks calm but his eyes glitter unnaturally. My insides feel like glass that is about to shatter.

"My mother cooks nothing but eggs. Every day, only eggs. Never rice and meat like she should," Rodwin says in a high, thin voice. He abruptly sits down. He refuses to look in my direction.

He's been coached and is parroting exactly what his father has told him to say. My heart aches for him. I want to embrace him and tell him that I don't hold any of this against him. But I must remain silent. I keep my face blank and tightly control my emotions.

The room is so quiet that I can hear flies buzzing in and out the open windows. All eyes are back on the judge.

"What more is there to say? Divorce this abominable woman!" The judge slaps the papers down on his desk in righteous anger.

Mansoor stands. He loosens his tie with one hand. His carefully groomed hair looks disheveled as he runs his hand nervously over the top of his head. "Divorce? I don't want a divorce. She is the mother of my children."

There is a moment of stunned silence in the courtroom. It is a stillness that vibrates out of balance. Something is wrong, dangerously wrong. The court recorder looks up at the judge with a startled expression. Jimi and Bob feel the confusion in the air but don't know exactly what is happening.

The judge looks intently at me, then back to Mansoor. He says nothing for a long moment. I know what he is thinking. *He's not in his right mind. What man would continue living with a woman who commits such disgusting acts?*

I sense a change in the atmosphere of the courtroom. In that split second, I feel a flicker of hope. I reach for Jimi's hand. The judge may now be aware that Mansoor is not a sane man. He looks in my direction with a brief but definite look of compassion. He can see what a dismal future awaits me if I return to Mansoor's custody. My life would be pinched out like a flickering candlewick and Mansoor would never have to account for my sudden demise.

"I decree that this woman be sent back to her father's house. That is my final ruling." Relief causes tears to well up. I wipe them. I'm too stunned to speak.

The judge confers with the clerk for a moment, then requests Mansoor to come and sign papers that release me to leave the country. Mansoor reluctantly obeys. I can see in his posture that he is signing under duress. The judge stands and walks out the door behind his desk. It is over. I am to be sent back to America by court decree. Mansoor and Rodwin leave the courtroom. The Olds and I return to the parking lot.

"That judge used the wisdom of Solomon," Bob says on the drive back.

"What do you mean?" Jimi asks.

"He can't let the husband or the precepts of Islam lose face by calling the husband insane. A man's word against a mere woman must always prevail. On the other hand, he didn't want to send Shareen to an early grave at the hands of such a husband."

"So he sends me home in disgrace. My parents will be thrilled that I can use the airline ticket waiting at the TWA office." My elation is tempered by the knowledge that my father paid for three tickets. Rodwin and Shadwin will not be using their tickets at this time. But I cling to the hope that it will only be a matter of months before we are reunited.

"The judge was smart to make Mansoor sign the papers giving you permission to leave the country," Jimi adds in a thoughtful tone.

"Yeah, Mansoor would change his mind if he could. Now it's too late."

Bob turns his head to speak to me in the back seat of the car. "I guess y'all must have extravagant Easter celebrations, what with your fixation on eggs, Shareen."

His joke breaks the tension hanging over us. I laugh for the first time in weeks. But the pain of hearing Rodwin recite that ridiculous claim about eggs will stay with me for a lifetime.

Now, the days rush by as I make plans to leave Iran. It has been six years since I left the United States, and I am eager to return. First, I must visit Ginger and Ruthann to say good-bye and thank them for their friendship. We sit on the cushions in their living room and drink tea. Simon and Garfunkle's "Bridge Over Troubled Waters" is playing on the stereo. I will always associate this song with my last days in Teheran.

One last detail. I need an exit visa. Jimi and I visit the Ministry of Interior. I explain my business and hand the clerk my American passport.

"Come back tomorrow, Madame," he advises.

The next morning, Jimi and I hail a taxi and tell the driver to take us to the center of Teheran.

I approach the counter and speak to the same clerk. "Is my visa ready?"

"Not yet," he says rather ambiguously. "We need your Persian passport."

I fish around in my handbag and pull out the red-covered Iranian passport issued nine years ago in California. I hand it to him and ask that he return my American passport.

"I need it to enter America." I smile politely.

"You need only an Iranian passport, Khanoum." He smiles politely back at me. "We have destroyed your useless American passport."

Feeling angry and outraged, Jimi and I go immediately to the American Embassy and report the loss of my passport. The Consular General is not surprised. This has obviously happened before. He issues me a new passport and advises me to hide it until I'm out of Iran. But I still need an exit visa. No traveler can leave Iran without an exit visa, police background check, and in the case of women, a husband or father's written approval.

Jimi and I go back the Ministry of Interior every day and ask for my visa. We patiently sit on the hard wooden bench and wait for my name to be called. Weeks pass.

One morning, Jimi looks out the window of our taxi and sees a tall, husky blond American striding along the sidewalk.

"Bruno!" she calls.

He stops and looks in our direction.

"Over here." Jimi waves her hand outside the taxi. I request the driver to pull alongside the curb.

"Bruno, you're just the man we need. Come with us to the Ministry of Interior." He ducks his six-foot-four inch frame inside the small taxi and grins agreeably.

"How can I help you?"

"We need a man to intervene for us." Jimi briefly updates him on the recalcitrant clerks who won't issue me an exit visa.

"Bruno's not only an ex-Naval officer, but once played football for USC," Jimi informs me. "He and his wife are missionaries living in an isolated village in the north of Iran. What a blessing to find him in Teheran this day," she adds.

Bruno goes with us to the Ministry of Interior. He marches up to the counter. "Give me her passport and visa now."

The clerk's face registers surprise followed by alarm. His eyes measure Bruno's height and shoulder width. "One moment." He walks to the back to confer with a heavyset, bearded man. They both stare at Bruno.

I hold my breath. Jimi and I have tried every day for two weeks to no avail. I don't think they will comply just because he is a male.

I'm wrong. The clerk returns with a tight smile on his face. He reaches under the counter and hands an envelope to Bruno.

Bruno says, *Mowchakarem*, thank you very much, in perfect Farsi.

The visa was there all along. They just refused to give it to me. Why? Out of spite? But they don't even know me. "Why, why?" I ask Jimi.

"Just praise God, honey."

We thank Bruno, then drop him off where we picked him up. Jimi and I return home to pack my bags.

Jimi arranges with Mansoor for me to have a farewell lunch with my sons at the American Commissary Restaurant. Rodwin and Shadwin arrive wearing white shirts and long trousers, their thick dark hair slicked back with water. As we sit down at a large round table I reminisce about the good times we had at the American Embassy. Every Fourth of July, the staff hosted a barbeque for all Americans living in Teheran. Not as much fun, but more important, were the free vaccinations against cholera and other life-threatening diseases. I smile as I remember how Rodwin ran out of the Embassy when he saw the needle in the doctor's hand. I caught him in the gardens and took him back inside.

Now, we are here eating our last hamburger together. They don't realize that they will not see their mother for a long time. I'm hoping it won't be more than six months. Surely, it will take less than a year for Mansoor to admit he can't support them. Then he will send Rodwin and Shadwin to me in America. This thought makes this last meal together bearable.

Roberta Dawson joins us at this farewell lunch along with two middle-aged missionary ladies who are in town to visit Jimi and Bob Old. I shake hands with Doctor Flora Colby and Miss Hazel Kleintop, never suspecting that I will one day live with them in their villa outside Jerusalem.

I'm totally focused on Rodwin and Shadwin. Shadi can't finish his chocolate milkshake, so his brother polishes it off. They both finish their hamburger and fries. Roberta takes pictures so that I will have a memento of this day. I kiss and hug the boys for one last time. My emotions are conflicted. Sorrow and elation do not sit comfortably together. But hope for the future gives me courage to act normally.

Part Two

Our feet shall stand within thy gates, O Jerusalem

Psalm 122:2

Israel, 1969

By a peculiar circumstance of fate, I am *going up* to Jerusalem, *aliyah*, as I later learn it is said in Hebrew. Jerusalem sits high above the coastal plain of Tel Aviv on the west side and above the Jordan Valley on the east. Hence the term going up. The airplane ticket provided by my father is scheduled for a stopover in Tel Aviv, something I would never have arranged on my own. But having the opportunity to visit this raw, energetic yet ancient land, I determine to see as much as possible in one week.

I weep silent but copious tears during the entire flight from Teheran to Tel Aviv. The stewardess discreetly serves my drinks and meal without any acknowledgment of my distress. Arriving at Ben Gurion Airport, weak and drained of emotion, I look forward to booking into the pension that Jimi and Bob have arranged for me in the Old City of Jerusalem. Traveling with a tight budget, having only one hundred U.S. dollars in my purse, I take a public bus from the airport to Jerusalem.

Though technically still in the Middle East, I discern a different mentality in the local population when the bus driver gets out of his seat and helps me heft my heavy suitcase up the stairs, shoving it under my seat. I have to rest my feet on the part of the suitcase that sticks out, but that doesn't bother me. I note this new phenomenon, mentally comparing the behavior of the Israelis with that of Iranians, rather than judging everything by American standards. An Iranian bus driver would never leave his position behind the wheel. Furthermore, there would be no space in a packed Iranian bus to hold a suitcase.

Leaving the orange groves surrounding Tel Aviv, the bus winds upward (aliyah) on the highway to Jerusalem. The terrain changes dramatically from warm and semitropical to mountains sparsely covered with pine and fir. The citrus and avocado trees giving way to low mountains remind me of my childhood in Los Angeles. All similarities end as I witness the rusted, burnt-out tanks lying alongside the highway in mute testimony to the bitterly fought battle for Jerusalem in 1967.

I reach Jerusalem just as the late afternoon sun gently bathes the luminous white stone buildings in its soft glow. It is this effect that gives the city its famous name, Jerusalem of Gold.

Modern Jerusalem resembles a provincial town in France, with its red-tiled roofs, window boxes of geraniums, and laundry hanging from balconies. But, when I enter the Old City through Jaffa Gate, I feel I'm back in Iran. Organized chaos fills the narrow plaza in front of the Citadel of David. Tourists head down dark alleyways into the bazaars. A donkey, carrying a wooden pallet of donut-like sesame rolls, is led by a young boy who looks no older than my nine-year-old son Rodwin.

Begeleh! Begeleh! He shouts in a high thin voice.

I have a bed waiting for me at Christ Church Hospice inside Jaffa Gate. Literally a bed in a dormitory. This, plus breakfast and dinner, will cost less than five dollars a day. Jimi and Bob always stay here (albeit in a private room) when they visit the Holy Land, and they insisted I stay there on my journey homeward to California. The Church of England built the church and hospice in the late nineteenth century. Pilgrims like myself have come here for more than a hundred years.

I awake the next morning to the familiar sound of the *muezzin* calling the faithful to prayer. What isn't familiar is the ringing of church bells from the nearby Armenian Quarter. At breakfast, I learn that the Old City is divided into quarters: Moslem, Jewish, Christian, and Armenian.

The hospice dining room is a friendly place with large wooden tables and benches that seat eight guests. I have my first bacon and eggs in six years. The bacon lies limply on my plate, half cooked, with the rind and a bit of pig hair still attached. It reminds me that I am not in England or America, but still in the Middle East. Of course the Muslim cook in the kitchen never eats pork himself. Neither do the Jews. Only the unfortunate tourists have to face such fare first thing in the morning.

After breakfast, I go out to explore the Old City. From the front gate of Christ Church I turn right and enter the souk, where I will buy my daily lunch of dates and a fresh sesame bagel. The narrow lane twisting downward into the heart of the Muslim quarter is lined with shops selling silver, gold, carpets, and ancient artifacts. I stop to admire a necklace made of fine turquoise stones. I go in to inquire about the price, even though I have no money to spend on such luxury items. The shopkeeper offers me a cup of Turkish coffee, which I accept guiltily, knowing I'm not going to buy. Eventually, we get around to bargaining.

"One hundred dollars."

I counter with fifty dollars. Right away I know the beautiful necklace is not real turquoise even though the shopkeeper swears on his mother's head that it is the purest quality of stone. A similar necklace, bought in Iran, a country famous for its turquoise, would cost hundreds of dollars. I leave the shop empty handed. The Arab shopkeeper says *m'salami*, go in peace. He knows a less informed American or European tourist will soon come in and buy his fake jewelry.

I spend the morning wandering around the various bazaars. Close to midday, I come out onto a large plaza. A plaque tells me this is the Western Wall, popularly called the Wailing Wall. I can see how that name came into being. Crowds of men and women, separated by a low metal railing, are converging on the Wall, all that remains of Solomon's Temple. The men, dressed in the long black coats and fur hats of the European Jewish *shtetl*, recite prayers as they sway and bob up and down in a stiff manner. The women, wearing head scarves and long sleeves, lean their heads against the ancient stones and weep as they make their silent petitions to Heaven. I feel immediate empathy, having cried more in the past six years than in the previous twenty. I'm wearing a long-sleeved blouse. All I lack is the scarf. Crossing the plaza to the women's side of the wall, I see a table full of scarves. I borrow one and tie it under my chin.

The cracks around the heavy stones in the wall are filled with tiny slips of paper filled with petitions to God. I reach in my handbag, take out a pen, tear a piece of paper off an envelope, and scribble a prayer that I will soon be reunited with my sons. I reach as high as I can, standing on tiptoe to insert it into a crevice. Then I lean my head against the cool stones. Waves of emotion sweep over me, causing my shoulders to tremble, then shake, as sobs tear through my throat. I'm not prepared for this public show of emotion and hide my face. But no one is looking at me. This is what happens at the Western Wall. *Rachel weeping for her children, and cannot be comforted, for they are not.*

Four

From the plaza at the Western Wall I head for the nearby Dung Gate. Outside the Old City walls, I gaze across the Kidron Valley. Immediately across is the mausoleum of Absalom, King David's rebellious son. If it were David's burial place, I would navigate the treacherous path down the wadi and up the other side. But Absalom does not capture my interest.

I lift my eyes and in the distance see the Garden of Gethsemane on the lower slope of the Mount of Olives. This I must see up close. On foot, I follow the winding road. The sun is now almost overhead, and the heat is growing. Perspiration trickles down my neck into my collar. I wish I had a cold soft drink. An old Franciscan monk sits on a stool at the entrance to the grove of olive trees where Christ pleaded with his Father to take the cup of suffering from him. I nod to the monk, who barely acknowledges my presence. I step into a pleasant coolness that only a Middle Eastern garden can produce. I stop to breathe the fragrance of the twisted, gnarled olive trees. It's an earthy smell of wood and leaves mixed with something bitter. The unripe olives?

I no longer hear the roar of traffic from the road to Jericho. I'm alone. I take my Bible out of my bag and read again how Jesus wept and prayed here while his disciples slept from sheer fatigue. Right here, the traitor Judas kissed his master on the cheek. I find it hard to place those treacherous events in this peaceful, tranquil garden. After some minutes I leave, comforted but not spiritually aware enough to appreciate the full impact of the garden.

I continue wandering around in the Old City, feeling more and more at home, ignoring the dusty cobblestones, donkey droppings, and bits and pieces of trash. Even the reeking sheep market does not adversely affect me. I sense this reaction is partially filtered by the six years spent in Teheran. Yet, there is something else happening here. I'm happy, truly happy. No, it is not happiness. It's more a peaceful feeling. A sense of belonging. I don't stop to analyze why a freshly minted Christian, recently divorced from a Muslim, would feel at home among the Jews.

I spend the afternoon climbing on the ancient walls, built by the Turkish Sultan, Sulieman the Great, in the sixteenth century. They are broad enough in some places to drive a chariot on them. I start at Damascus Gate, so named because it faces the famous city of Damascus. Then I head toward St. Stephen's Gate, named for the first Christian martyr. I continue on top of the wall to Jaffa Gate, where I encounter a lone Israeli soldier on guard duty. He is wearing olive green fatigues that look like American army fatigues, and probably are American surplus. He holds an Uzi in the crook of his right arm while leaning on a parapet. The expression on his face is one of acute boredom.

"Hi," I say.

"Shalom," he replies. He is tanned, with dark hair and blue eyes.

There is a pause. Neither of us knows how or if we should continue this conversation.

"Where are you from?" he asks in heavily accented English.

"California," I reply with no intention of telling him that I have just been expelled from Iran.

He nods and smiles as if he has heard good things about California.

Without preamble, I blurt out to this stranger, "I love Jerusalem. Wish I could stay here forever." I had no idea I would say that. But I immediately know it is true. This is my city. This is my home. This revelation breaks into my consciousness like cold water on a parched tongue. I feel ineffable joy and peace, even as I speak these surprising words to the soldier, who looks younger than me by at least five years.

"Here," he says stretching out his arms to offer me his Uzi. "You take this and stay here. I will go to California."

We both laugh to break the tension of heartfelt intentions that we know cannot be fulfilled. At least not at this time or in this way.

I decide to visit the Galilee on my last two days in Israel, so I reserve a seat in a six-passenger touring car that operates out of Jaffa Gate. The driver is Armenian, born and raised in Jerusalem. He drives north through the hill country of Judea and Samaria, rather than take the desert route through Jericho. I'm glad to avoid the heat of the Jordan Valley. We stop for a picnic lunch near the village of Dotan.

"This is where Joseph's brothers threw him into a pit, then sold him to a passing caravan of Ishmaelites for twenty pieces of silver," says the driver-cum-tour-guide.

I eat my egg salad sandwich and try to fathom Joseph's despair. I can relate to this story of family betrayal.

"How do things turn out for Joseph?" I ask our guide with more than a little curiosity.

"I see you don't know your Bible," he replies.

I smile, not taking offense. I love the book of Isaiah and parts of the New Testament, but I'm not going to tell him that.

"The caravan took Joseph to Egypt and sold him to Potiphar's household. Being the good Jewish boy that he was, he resisted the advances of his master's wife. Nevertheless, he ended up in leg irons."

"Does he get out?" By now, I'm relating to the story in a painfully personal manner. "Joseph not only makes it out of the dungeon, but rises to the position of Viceroy over all Egypt."

"I bet that made his brothers sick with envy," I say with satisfaction.

The guide stood to shake the crumbs off his lap. "We have to get moving. You can read the rest of the story in the book of Genesis."

Reaching the Sea of Galilee, or Kinneret as it is also called because of its harp shape, I check into the Scottish Hospice. This guest house was built by the Church of Scotland originally as a hospital. After Israel became a nation in 1948 and built its own hospitals, the Scots turned it into a hospice for pilgrims.

The four buildings, built of lava stone, are scattered throughout the lush, almost tropical gardens. It reminds me of the British Raj that I read about in Passage to India.

From my verandah, I look across the water to the hazy outline of the Golan Heights on the other side. When checking in, I am told by the desk clerk that it is only a one-hour drive to Damascus. When I ask if I could take a bus there, he only laughs.

"Don't you know Syria and Israel are enemies?"

I want to swim, but of course I don't have a swimsuit. While in Iran, I didn't dare wear a swimsuit. I can't afford to buy one here, having only a hundred dollars for the entire journey, but I can walk barefoot along the edge of the water.

Some distance outside of Tiberias, I come upon a young fisherman tending his nets.

"Could you row me out into the lake?" I ask politely.

"Two pounds," he counters. (Israeli currency is still in pounds according to the British system. It will be some years before the shekel becomes the official currency.)

I mentally convert the two pounds into four dollars and nod my assent. He put aside his nets, then pushes the small wooden boat into the water. I wade in up to my knees, holding my skirt high, then climb into the boat. He rows out some distance, then starts the outboard motor.

If I thought this would be a spiritual experience as in Jerusalem, I'm soon disappointed. Alone out on the waters, the fisherman, no more than a teenager, stops the engine and moves over to my side of the boat. He puts a hand on my knee and pulls me close to him.

"What are you doing?" I push his hand away as I judge the distance from shore. Can I swim that far?

Still smiling, he gently tries again.

I realize that my request to be taken out in his boat gave him the wrong signal. He thinks this is what I expect. Israel is different from Iran in its attitudes toward women, but it is still the Middle East. I can see in his eyes, though, that he is not prepared to force himself on me.

"Let's go back. Now." I say in a commanding tone.

He puts both arms around my shoulders and embraces me. I don't resist. Let him have the comfort of a hug, I tell myself.

The next day, while sitting in the passengers' lounge waiting to continue my journey back to California, I idly watch a cat playing with a mouse. The mouse is limp, but not dead. The cat backs off and gives it time to run, then pounces again. After playing with the mouse a moment, he lets it go. Then catches it and bats it back and forth between its paws. I feel like that mouse and Mansoor is the cat. I shudder with relief that I am safely out of his grasp.

I look forward to hours spent on the plane. Between one destination and the next I need make no decisions. No demands are made of me. I like the sensation of suspended animation. The terrible weight of leaving Rodwin and Shadwin lifts during travel. Plus the nagging fear that I may be misjudging Mansoor's resolve to keep the boys is temporally suspended in mid-flight.

Five

Flying over the Atlantic I have time to dwell on the changes that I will face back in America. While I was in Iran, my father had been transferred to Las Vegas to manage the one and only dairy plant in that city. Then he and my mother divorced after thirty-five years of marriage. My life has drastically changed, but so has theirs. I don't know what to expect, but I'm definitely not returning to the happy ambience of my childhood in Los Angeles. Neither are my children having the happy childhood that I once envisioned for them. But it will get better, I reassure myself. It won't be long before Mansoor sends them to me in America. I repeat this over and over, it won't be long.

My mother picks me up at McCarren Airport. We hug and kiss awkwardly, aware of a separation of more than six years. She avoids any mention of Rodwin and Shadwin to spare my feelings. Then she drives down the Strip to show me the town.

"Well, what do you think of it?"

"Gee, it's real pretty." Sensory overload is what I'm thinking.

We pass the Sahara Hotel, which glitters as if diamonds were glued to its exterior.

She turns off the Strip onto Rancho Road. We pass through a wealthy neighborhood where I know she doesn't live.

"The McGuire sisters live there." She points a finger to the left. "Red Skelton over there."

We pass a riding stable next to a park with a large duck pond. "Kim used to board her pony there."

My little sister is now grown up and too big for ponies. She was only fourteen when I went to Iran.

I settle in with my mother and sister in the three-bedroom house on Avalon Circle. It feels good to be back in America, but living in Las Vegas is surreal. Trying to act as normal as possible, I attend several of the local churches. Las Vegas has hundreds of churches to choose from, but I don't feel comfortable in any of them because my limited religious experience has been in an informal home setting.

I'm still in touch with my friends in Teheran, and they in turn keep me up to date with as much detail as they can glean about Rodwin and Shadwin. I write to Rodwin and he writes back, but his letters tell me little. I'm giving Mansoor six months to realize he can't support a family and then send the boys to me in America. I'm still convinced this will happen.

In the meantime, Shan and Dick Dryer write from Iran suggesting that I visit a home fellowship in Las Vegas that they know about. They give me the name and phone number of an ex-show girl.

Elaine's large, well kept home is just two streets off the Strip in a quiet neighborhood. She is thirty-something, with short dark hair and luminous eyes. She is shorter than I, which surprises me. I expected a showgirl to be six feet tall.

"I was a dancer and singer, not a showgirl," she says, seeming to read my mind.

The fellowship that meets in her house is composed of various Christians from all backgrounds: Baptist, Pentecostal, Methodist. Elaine is from a Jewish background. They all have in common the experience of the baptism of the Holy Spirit. It seems like eons since

I have spoken in tongues, and then it was only once. I'm shy and unsure of myself. I mostly listen since I don't know any of the choruses they sing so enthusiastically.

The weeks and months pass. I continue going twice a week to the home fellowship. Actually, we meet in Elaine's home only on Thursday evening. Sunday morning we meet in the Odd Fellow's Hall just off Fremont Street. Pastor Glade Smith and his wife Helen always stay after the service to pray for anyone who requests it. By now, I'm beginning to feel uncomfortable because I can't sing and praise God in tongues like the rest of them do. So, one Sunday, I timidly approach Helen.

"I've received the baptism of the Holy Spirit, in Iran, but I don't feel free to raise my arms and praise God."

Helen puts her hand gently on my shoulder and begins to pray in soft tones. This woman used to play the piano in the Baptist Church until she and her husband received the Baptism in the Holy Spirit and were asked to leave. Her demeanor and tone are still more Baptist than Pentecostal.

She has said only a few words when I feel my arms shooting straight up in the air as if they were pulled by strings. I am startled because this happens without my volition. I hear myself praying in some unknown language. Then a sense of peace supplants my initial misgivings. I feel energized by one simple touch from this quiet and unassuming woman. I intuit that it is the Holy Spirit passing from Helen to me, and I look at her with gratitude and awe.

She smiles and says, "Praise God."

That's it. I no longer have any inhibitions about raising my hands in worship.

I hang a poster in my bedroom that says, *If I forget you, O' Jerusalem, let my right hand lose its cunning*. I see no way I can return to Jerusalem, but the inner yearning never leaves, even though it is by necessity on a back burner.

My father gives me his old '55 Chevy with big fish fins on the side.

"It runs OK, but I wouldn't advise driving it out of town," he says as he hands me the keys.

I don't tell him that I'm planning on driving to Waco, Texas, in the near future. I find Las Vegas is not my cup of tea. I'm only marking time here, waiting for my boys, and waiting for that mystical call to return to Jerusalem.

Of course, like most people who grew up in Los Angeles, I had never heard of Waco. But my friends in Teheran know of a little church there. The pastor, Jack Locker, is the best Bible teacher in the West, they write me. They suggest I move there.

"Wacko," I tell my sister and Mom. "I'm moving to Wacko." On the serious side, I do think a small town in Texas will be a better place to raise two boys than Las Vegas.

I pack my clothes, kiss my mother and sister good-bye, and drive in the fin-tailed Chevy across Nevada, Arizona, New Mexico, and half of Texas. My father's advice, as usual, is right on target. Steam is pouring out of the engine as I pull into a gas station in Waco. I call him to tell him I arrived safely in Waco.

"O Lord, give me strength," replies my long-suffering father.

Pastor Jack Locker and his wife Edna greet me as if I'm their daughter. In fact, they have no children, just a Great Dane. They live in the small parsonage next to the church but own a two-story wooden house a block away.

"Sharon, honey, the house is yours as long as you want."

Their hospitality amazes me. I'm a virtual stranger and they give me the keys to their house. Texas is another country. They speak English with a lilt and emphasize different syllables. Edna says PO-lice or UM-brella. I'm told that my accent is no longer American. In

Iran, I needed to speak with distinct enunciation like the British in order to be understood. Not only is my speech pattern foreign, but I also dress differently. I wear mini-skirts or maxi-skirts, whereas the women of this church wear their hem lines precisely one inch below the knee.

The church, called Grace Gospel, is an old wooden building that lists to one side. It has hard wooden pews, an upright piano, and a pulpit. They sing old-fashioned hymns like "Bringing in the Sheaves" and "The Old Rugged Cross." I love the songs, not only the words but the melodies.

On Sunday evening, the teenagers lead the worship with their own musical group. They write original music for the psalms. Instead of picking up a hymnal, the congregation opens their Bible and sings from the words written in the King James Version.

I like everything about these people, even Sister Rose, a little lady with white hair in a bun who stands up at the beginning of every service and relates how Jesus saved her. To my ears, everything she says is fresh and original.

Waco will be a good place to raise my sons, I decide. These people are not concerned with material things or outward appearance. By the end of my first week, I have a job in an insurance company processing claims. Before work, I study the Bible every morning with Pastor Locker. We spend three months on the life of King David. There is a worship service four times a week with lots of singing and good biblical exegesis that draws a number of students from nearby Baylor University.

It's here in Waco that I learn about spiritual discernment. It all begins one evening when a redhaired woman sitting in a back pew interrupts the sermon with an impassioned speech about her unfaithful husband. "I'm going to kill myself," she screams, then runs out the back door.

No one says or does anything. Don't they care that this poor woman is about to commit suicide? I run out and catch up with her on the sidewalk. I try to calm her down, but she is sobbing hysterically by now. I don't know what else to do, so I write my phone number on a piece of paper and ask her to call me when she gets home. Later that night, she telephones. For two hours, I am forced to listen to a vivid account of her husband's lewd behavior.

The next morning I confide to Edna, the pastor's wife, that I feel overwhelmed and unable to help the redhaired lady.

"Sharon, dear, she's been pulling this stunt for years. We've tried to counsel her many times, but she refuses to change. Pay her no mind. She used to be a lion tamer, you know."

Then, one Sunday morning, I notice a stranger sitting next to Edna. She is an American missionary recently come from a tour of duty in Africa, I learn later. During the part of the service where anyone can stand and give a testimony or praise report, this middle-aged woman strides up to the pulpit and begins to speak.

She says all the right things, like praise God . . . isn't Jesus wonderful. But it doesn't sound right coming from her mouth. She smiles a ghastly grin that causes the hair on the back of my neck to stand up. I feel a strong urge to run out of the church. I sense something evil is happening, but everybody is sitting calmly in their seats. Am I imagining this? I will myself to stay put in the pew by grabbing the wooden bench with both hands. But the desire to flee is still there.

The visiting missionary is preaching a sermon. Before long, Pastor Locker stands up and shouts, "Stop! Now!"

I've never heard him use this harsh tone before, and I'm riveted to the pew by the tension in the air. She stares back at him with bright shining eyes. I sense a battle of wills between them. She smiles her mirthless grin and returns to her seat. The silence in the church is electric. After the service, I can hardly wait to ask Edna what that was all about.

"Sharon, honey, this poor woman is possessed by evil spirits. She showed up at our house on Saturday. Said God wanted her to preach Sunday morning. Jack told her he does the preaching here."

"The minute she opened her mouth, I felt cold, clammy fear up and down my spine. Her smile is ghastly."

"You're beginning to discern spirits, honey."

My education in spiritual discernment began with the encounter with the lion-tamer's bogus, but harmless, outburst during the service. I'm beginning to understand the difference between her behavior and that of the missionary recently returned from Africa. The first woman sought only to disrupt. The second woman tried to usurp power and authority from the pastor. The redhead whose husband was a flagrant philanderer, or so she claimed, evoked my pity as just another messed-up human being. On the other hand, the missionary raised the hackles on my neck because she was possessed with pure evil.

I didn't know it then, but these exercises in spiritual discernment were to play a large role in my encounters in Jerusalem in the years ahead. Edna and Jack Locker's tutelage would turn out to be more valuable than gold.

I have been in Waco about six months when I hear that Shan and Dick Dryer, my friends from Teheran, are coming for a visit. Because they are also friends of Pastor Locker, they plan to spend a week in the same house I'm living in. I've never forgotten how they gently pointed me away from the cult teachings of Edgar Cayce. Now, I eagerly wait to hear firsthand news about Rodwin and Shadwin.

During our first supper together, Shan senses my state of mind and gently remarks, "Your boys are doing real good."

"You can be proud of them," Dick adds as I pass him the rolls.

Then there is a long pause as they go about the business of filling the plates of their young son and daughter.

"Mansoor seems to have a second wife," Shan begins in a hesitant voice.

"Seems?" I reply, my fork in mid air.

"Well, she's not exactly a servant. Neither is she a full-fledged wife.

"What do you mean?" I'm stunned. Surely Mansoor would have written to me if he had married again, if for no other reason than to gloat.

"She apparently is hired to look after Rodwin and Shadwin and the house," Shan replies.

"But she accompanies Mansoor and the boys when they make family visits," adds Dick as he helps himself to the fried chicken.

"I see." I try not to show that I'm upset with this news. Mansoor has obviously hired a housekeeper who is less than a wife but more than a servant. It means he is coping with the challenge of raising a ten-year-old and a four-year-old without me. Icy dread sits in my stomach like a stone. I anticipated that he would be forced to give in and send Rodwin and Shadwin to America by the end of the first year. I now sense this is not going to happen.

"By the way, did you know that Chris recently married?" Sensing my distress, Shan is trying to change the subject not knowing that she is adding to it.

"Is the bride anybody I know?" I reply. My mind is reeling. This is the man I daydream about, the CIA agent that I vowed never to see again. Did Shan and Dick know about my affair? I don't think so. It's painful to learn that this man's life (like Mansoor's) is going on without me.

I don't recognize the name Shan gives me. To cover my confusion and hurt, I pass the platter of chicken again. All my dreams lie shattered on the kitchen table amid the remains of Sunday dinner.

To hide my distress, I get up and fuss with the strawberry shortcake in the fridge. Acknowledging my delusions to myself is one thing. To admit them to others is something I can't do at this point. If I thought the worst of my ordeal was over, I now know it is not. That huge chunk of me that is missing, the day-to-day duty and tasks of mothering, is not to be restored anytime soon.

Life in Waco goes on. I don't fit in with the women my age. I'm single. Therefore I don't have much in common with the married couples. In my late twenties, I'm also too old for the high school and college crowd.

I look to Edna for direction. As the pastor's wife, she must walk a delicate balance among her husband's little flock. For friendship she turns to two women who don't attend her husband's church: Jewel, a widow who works at the VA hospital; and Betsy, a transplanted New Yorker married to a wealthy Waco businessman. The three have lunch once or twice a month.

One day Edna asks me if I will drive her friend Jewel to Dallas that weekend. Jewel has trouble with her night vision.

"Sure," I reply. Edna knows my weekends are free.

Jewel and I hit it off immediately. We drive to Dallas munching on the sandwiches she has prepared. She tells me about her life and her work with the mental patients at the VA hospital. She talks and I drive during the two hours it takes us to get to Dallas.

"José used to spit on everybody. The nurses, attendants, even me. One day, I asked him what would really make him happy. Would you believe, Sharon, all he wanted was a real, good Mexican meal? So, I arranged for two strong orderlies to accompany José and me to a nearby Mexican restaurant. He ate and ate. When he could eat no more, I asked if he wanted dessert. He finished a bowl of vanilla ice cream. He's been a docile patient ever since."

I don't tell Jewel much about my life in Iran, preferring to hear her stories. Betsy joins us for dinner now and then, but she has a family and social life to attend to. But Betsy teaches me what it means to have compassion for animals. At any given time, she has four or five stray dogs living in her home in the most elegant part of Waco. She routinely carries dog food and water in the trunk of her car and feeds every stray dog she sees. Many years later in Israel, I will carry on Betsy's love of animals.

I'm only marking time in Waco. I work at an insurance company but have no ambition to be promoted from my position as an entry-level clerk. I attend all services at church, absorbing all the spiritual lessons I can. I occasionally drive across Texas with Jewel to attend lectures in Dallas or Houston. But my heart is not here. I yearn to be the mother of my children. I want to put Rodwin and Shadwin to bed at night, tuck them in, pray with them, or tell them a story. I want to help Rodwin with his homework and teach Shadi how to tie his shoe laces. I want to hold my little boy in my lap and smell the sweet animal sweat that rises off his thin neck after play.

Two years pass in this way. I send letters to Teheran and boxes of clothes. I worry they won't have enough clean underwear. Betsy gives me cartons of books, children's classics, that I pack up and ship to Rodwin. The political climate in Iran is gradually changing. Revolution is now a possibility, though the press in America seems to think the Shah cannot be deposed.

Then I get a call from my father in Las Vegas. He asks me to come back to help my younger brother, Patrick, a police detective, who is going through a difficult divorce. He is trying to get custody of both of his children and needs me there to be the babysitter. I agree to help out.

Flying over the mammoth desert between Texas and Las Vegas, I try to recall what I know about my brother's soon to be ex-wife. She has long black hair, blue eyes, and an enviable figure. Before I left for Waco she gave birth to a blond, blue-eyed son. They named him Michael. She recently gave birth to a daughter they named Tori.

The plane taxies down the tarmac. I can see the hotels on the Strip from the window. Las Vegas is an anomaly. I don't think there is another city in the world like it. My brother meets me at McCarren Airport and, as we drive down Las Vegas Boulevard, I find the excess of bad taste so over the top that it makes me laugh. Champagne brunches for three dollars. Prime rib for five dollars. Show girls with fannies like golden globes strut their stuff on billboards.

My brother and I don't say much to each other. We enjoy the comfortable companionship of siblings who love each other without envy or rivalry. There are six of us, three boys and three girls. We grew up with demonstrable love from our father. If our mother was not able to show her love, at least she ignored us all equally.

I listen with empathy as Patrick relates the details of his divorce. His wife, it turns out, is a pathological liar, much like Mansoor. He lived with her for three years and found he didn't know her at all.

Along with my own heartache and sense of injustice I now grieve for my brother when the judge gives his wife custody of their son and daughter. He is to pay child support and alimony and can only see them on the weekend. It is so unfair.

No longer needed in Las Vegas, I make preparations for the next stage of my life. I reluctantly accept the fact that Mansoor is not ready to send the boys to America. I will not be raising Rodwin and Shadwin in Waco. I think of Israel and how it is physically closer to Iran than the United States. I would only be a few hours away from them. So, in this frame of mind, I make plans to move to Jerusalem.

Six

Sitting on a low stone wall inside Jaffa Gate, I bask in the sights and sounds of Jerusalem. It is February 1974, and the Old City is just like I remembered it: Orthodox Jews in fur hats, their women in stylish wigs; Arab men in white or checkered *keffiyehs*; Franciscan monks in brown robes and sandals; nuns in full habit. Nothing has changed. Even the dust raised by their passing feet is infused with golden glints, like the glow I imagine shimmers around the feet of angels. I love this city—and now it's my new home.

To my left, in the shadow of the Citadel of David, is a wooden cart stacked with sesame buns. The vendor rolls up tiny strips of newspaper filled with zatar, a savory spice. It reminds me of the little packets of saffron that Mama Badri bought in the Teheran bazaar. I sit facing a tea room that also serves as a backgammon hall. Through the plate glass window I see Arab men drinking glasses of hot sweet tea as they toss the dice. I guess their women are home preparing lunch or doing laundry. Children in dark blue uniforms are heading for the nearby Armenian school. They carry their lunch in aluminum pails with tightly fitting lids. No sandwiches for these kids; it's rice, stew and vegetables. Rodwin has a similar three-tiered lunch pail. Everything reminds me of my sons. Do they miss me as much as I miss them?

I have enough money to stay one month at Christ Church Hospice. I know I need to find a job and a place to live before my money runs out. But I'm not anxious. God will open a door of employment.

After dinner, guests at Christ Church gather in the comfortably shabby sitting room for tea and biscuits. Most of them are middle-aged tourists from Britain or the United States. Outside the walls of the Hospice the atmosphere is pure Middle Eastern. Inside it is all British as the wife of the manager asks, "Milk or lemon in your tea, dear?"

I take milk with my Earl Gray and eat a chocolate covered cookie, or "digestive biscuit," as the English call it. Sitting in the area designated as the library, I look at the titles on the bookshelves.

"Find anything interesting?" A woman with short silver hair is sitting on the sofa opposite me. I can tell by her accent that she is from the American South. A slight man with ramrod straight posture is standing behind her. I assume he is her husband.

"I'm looking for some light bedtime reading," I reply. I'm shy and don't want to prolong the conversation, so I turn back to the bookshelf.

"I can't quite place your accent," the woman says in a congenial tone that ignores my reticence.

I fiddle with a strand of my long hair. "I'm American like you, but I've spent years in Iran." Why am I telling her this? I don't even know her name.

"I'm Toots Coleman and this is my husband, Pete," she replies as if she could read my thoughts. "We've just come from Teheran."

Now she has my attention. I lay my book on the table and turn to face her.

The woman with the odd name continues, "Our daughter lives in Addis Ababa. We stayed with her for a month and now we're on a tour of the Middle East."

I don't even know if I can pronounce Addis Ababa, even after just hearing it pronounced correctly. To play it safe I ask, "What is your daughter doing in Ethiopia?"

"She went there with the Peace Corps, fell in love with a man named Asafa, married him, and now she has three children."

"That's interesting," I say, but what I'm thinking is, should I now relate my sad tale of falling in love with Mansoor, being thrown out of Iran, and losing custody of my sons? I feel shame that only a mother who has lost her children can feel. So instead of revealing anything about myself, I ask this couple what they thought of Teheran.

Mr. Coleman replies to my question. "I'm retired Air Force. We travel on U.S. military planes on a space-available program. There was a chance to fly to Teheran, and we took it."

"Fascinating city," Toots says. "Charming people."

I nod, trying to remain noncommittal.

"What did you do in Teheran?" asks Pete.

Not wanting to go into my personal life with strangers, I tell them I had worked for the United Nations Development Program. I finish my tea, rise, and say good-night.

"Nice meeting you."

Mrs. Coleman surprises me by putting her arms around me in a long, warm hug. I stiffen, momentarily taken aback. Who are these people? I hardly know them. Why are they so friendly?

Later that week, Toots and Pete check out of Christ Church and rent an apartment overlooking the Arab souk. Pete enrolls in a study program on nearby Mount Zion to study Hebrew and archaeology. Toots opens a "salon" of sorts where people drop in day or night for good food, talk, and lots of hugs. I eventually warm up to her habit of hugging everyone every day. I can't, however, call her husband by his nickname "Honey" as she wants me to. It will always be Pete for me. It's hard enough to call her Toots (her given name is Freida).

It's here in their apartment that I meet Gideon Muller, a tall but stoop-shouldered man in his late fifties. He runs a tiny Bible shop built in the outer walls of the Hospice. He's an American Jew, now a believer in the Messiah Jesus. (Coincidentally, so is Toots. Pete is a mainline Protestant, West Point Officer, and a Southern gentleman of the old school). Gideon tells me he places a large Bible in his store window with the pages open to the New Testament.

"Every morning," he says, "An Orthodox Jew passes by on his way to pray at the Western Wall. Black hat, payote curls behind his ears, black coat . . . the works."

Gideon interrupts his story to explain the difference between the wide-brimmed black hat, the narrow-brimmed hat, and the various *kippot*.

"Their headgear," he explains like he is the professor and I'm the student, "denotes precise differences in religious philosophy and daily practices between the orthodox, ultra-orthodox, traditional, and secular. One day, this guy in the wide brimmed hat stops to read the Bible in the window. I oblige him by turning to a new page every morning."

I can see that Gideon relishes the idea of meeting this Hassid who wears the black coat and hat of the Polish shtetl.

"You wait and see, Sharona (he is the first person to Hebrewize my name). One day he will come in to argue with me." Gideon grins. "I can hardly wait."

I can't think of a more unlikely pair of debaters. Gideon is a reformed alcoholic and has been married and divorced five times.

"I don't even remember the last wife. I was drunk and we tied the hitch in Tijuana," he confides.

But now he is in recovery, and a born-again follower of Jeshua

HaMashiac. All kinds of people turn into his little shop. I, too, go to Gideon's shop and sit on the high stool before his counter.

"I need a job, and soon," I admit.

"You don't speak or write Hebrew?"

"Not a word."

"You like babies?"

My heart skips a beat. My own babies are growing up without me. Rodwin is now eleven and Shadwin is five. I telephone them as often as I can, but it isn't easy because there is no direct link between Israel and Iran. I have to go to the main Post Office on Jaffa Road. There I pay a prepaid amount to the long distance operator. She uses a convoluted plan that routes my call through the operator in Japan, then back to Pakistan, and on to Teheran. Most of the time, Mansoor answers and tells me the boys are outside playing or sleeping. I know he is lying, but even making contact with him is better than nothing.

I cautiously reply to Gideon's question. "What do you have in mind?"

"I know an English girl who works as a volunteer at the WIZO Baby Home in Bet HaKarem. She gets room and board and a small stipend."

"What about my lack of Hebrew?"

"No problem. These babies can't speak yet." He shrugs one shoulder in the Middle Eastern way.

"How do I meet her?" I ask.

"I'll introduce you."

By the end of the week, I'm wearing a pale green uniform with a large, white-bibbed apron. My title is *metapelet*, which means caregiver. I'm in charge of five toddlers from 7:00 A.M. to 6:00 P.M., six days a week. The WIZO (Women's International Zionist Organization) Baby Home is located in a pleasant, upper-middle-class neighborhood in west Jerusalem. It is an orphanage and nurses training school combined. I learn there is a category of nursing in Israel specifically oriented toward infants, something between a registered nurse and a practical nurse. At the Baby Home, young women who have finished their military service train to be special nurses in hospital pediatrics or in children's houses on kibbutzim. Fortunately for me, most of the nurses speak English. In fact, they are eager to practice what English they learned in high school.

Lesley and I share a room together in the student nurses' dormitory. Lesley is some years younger, blonde, tanned, and beautiful. Like me, she came to Israel as a tourist, fell in love with the country, and plans to stay here. We quickly become close friends, the friendship cemented by our mutual need to have work and a place to eat and sleep.

Unlike the student nurses who go to classes in the morning, Lesley and I report at 7:00 A.M. to the head nurse's office. The night duty nurse reads her chart and advises if any infant is sick or needs special attention. Then we go to our assigned rooms to wake our charges.

There are five metal cribs positioned against the walls. One entire wall is a sliding glass door that opens onto a verandah. Soft sunlight filters in through the branches of the leafy green trees that reach to the second floor, creating the effect of a jungle tree house. The babies in my assigned room range in age from fourteen to twenty-four months. They are sitting up, rubbing their eyes, eager to start their day.

Yoram, slightly retarded, is from a large orthodox family with twelve children. His mother is too ill to take care of him. Elinit's mother is in a mental hospital. Simira's mother is a prostitute in Tel Aviv. Rachel's mother is single and giving her up for adoption. Then there is Benny, the only true orphan. He was found abandoned in a trash bin during the war of Yom Kippur. Right away, something about

Benny appeals to me. He reminds me of my sons when they were this age, even thought there is no physical similarity. Benny has very curly black hair. Rodwin and Shadwin have straight brown hair.

I start with Yoram, stripping off his pee-soaked pajamas. (The head nurse believes plastic pants cause rashes.) I carry his warm, squiggling body to the little tub hung on the wall and give him a bath. When he is freshly diapered, smelling of baby lotion and powder, dressed in clean bibbed trousers and a shirt, I set him in his high chair. Then I strip his bed down to the plastic covered mattress and wipe all surfaces with a mixture of water and mild disinfectant. I remake his bed with clean linen fresh from the laundry. Then I go to Elinit's bed, then Rachel's, and so on until all are dressed and ready to eat.

Each one has his or her own high chair. I line them up like baby birds and spoon breakfast into their little open mouths. I take more time with Simira, whose tiny rosebud-shaped mouth can only handle the tip of the spoon. They obviously enjoy the mixture of mashed bananas, apples, and pure cream. The older ones get olives and tomatoes in addition to the fruit mixture. Olives for breakfast? I roll my eyes, but the toddlers seem to love it.

After breakfast is cleared away, it's playtime. Unlike a real mother who would have to do the housework, dishes, and laundry, I'm now free to play for several hours with the babies until lunch time. Lesley is performing the same routine in her room. We only see each other when we gather on the floor of the playroom.

After a week, I notice Benny doesn't crawl like the others. He can sit up and scoot across the floor on his bottom, but his legs lack muscle tension. When I hold him up by his arms, expecting him to push off with stiff legs, they go all rubbery. I'm troubled by Benny's legs and, after my shift is over, I have a long talk with the head nurse, Aliza.

"I named little Benny myself," Aliza tells me. "He was brought in when he was a few days old. My son's best friend had just been killed in the fighting. I named Benny after him."

I mentally calculate how old Benny is. The Yom Kippur war occurred in October of 1973. That makes him twelve months old.

"Who throws away a perfectly healthy male infant?" Aliza marvels. "He was found abandoned in a development town on the edge of the Negev desert. He could be Arab or Jew. We just don't know."

I don't say what I'm thinking, but to me Benny looks definitely to be of Arab stock. He has black hair, skin the color of milky coffee, and rather pronounced nostrils for one so young.

Aliza continues, "The student nurses decided among themselves that he must be an Arab *momzer*, bastard. And they weren't referring just to the circumstances of his birth. You can understand their attitude. I don't condone their taking it out on one so small, but there was an all-out attack on us from three sides. Egypt, Jordan, and Syria attacked simultaneously. These girls' fathers and brothers were dying." Aliza pauses and stares out the window at the lacy pattern caused by shadow and light through the tree branches.

"My son survived. His best friend did not. Little Benny received the necessary care, regular feedings, diaper changes . . . but no nurse picked him up to hold him or play with him. He lay on his back day and after day, and I'm afraid his leg muscles might be underdeveloped."

As Aliza speaks in her gentle voice, I know that I must do whatever is necessary to see that Benny learns to walk. My first act will be to take him to be examined by Dr. Colby.

I first met Dr. Colby in Teheran. She had been present at the farewell luncheon in the American commissary restaurant when I said good-bye to Rodwin and Shadwin. I focused only on the boys and paid scant attention to Dr. Colby. I thought I would never see her again. Now I receive a letter from Jimi Old telling me that Flora Colby is living in Bethany, an Arab village on the slopes of the Mount of Olives. *You must visit her*, Jimi insisted in her letter. On my next day off, I set out to find her.

The Arab bus station across from Damascus Gate is strewn with litter and packed with people. The station is carved out of a small bluff from the hill that Protestants call Calvary. My guide book tells me that archeologists place Calvary within the city gates and therefore the Holy Sepulcher, revered by the Catholics, is more likely to be the original Calvary. I don't give much thought to this dual universe of Catholics and Protestants, unaware that it will become a significant issue.

"Round trip to Bethany, please," I say to the ticket seller. Dr. Colby's rented villa is directly opposite Lazarus' tomb.

"Azaria?" he asks.

"Yes," I reply, knowing that the village is named after Lazarus, whom Jesus raised from the dead. *Lazaria, azaria*—I can hear the connection in the names.

I take my ticket and board the bus. The driver isn't in his seat, so I know we aren't leaving soon. I open my window for air because nearly every man on the bus is smoking, but diesel fumes combined with the cigarette smoke cause me to gag. I hold my hand over my mouth, hoping I won't throw up. The driver appears when the bus is filled to capacity, the aisles packed with standing passengers. A young man gets up and gives his seat to a woman with a toddler hanging onto her skirt. This is a courtesy I seldom saw in the United States.

We pull out of the station, take a left on Paratrooper Road, then right on the way to Jericho. Bethany is the first stop, twenty minutes from East Jerusalem. After getting off the bus, I locate the tomb of Lazarus. From here I see that the gate to Dr. Colby's villa is open.

I go into the garden, walk up to the front porch, and ring the bell. I had telephoned her from the Baby Home, so she is expecting me.

Dr. Colby answers the door herself. Her thinning gray hair is carefully wound around mesh rats that crown her face in an old fashioned coronet. She wears a white cotton blouse tucked into a blue skirt. The skin on her shins is a patchwork of scaly lace etched by the desert wind and sun. She wears cotton ankle socks and sensible low-heeled shoes.

"Come in, Sharon. How good to see you." She motions for me to take a seat in one of the wicker chairs that line the walls of her reception room. As she goes into the interior of the house to get me a glass of cold water, I take in my surroundings. There are windows on three sides like a solarium. She cultivates a large collection of bromeliads and succulents in brown clay pots. A yellow cat is sunning itself on a bookshelf. Another cat walks into the room, blinks at me, turns and leaves.

Dr. Colby returns with a metal tray before her. "Here, dear, have a drink of water from the same well that Mary and Martha drank from."

"Your cats are named Mary and Martha?"

She laughs, low and hearty. "I mean the Biblical Martha and Mary. Sisters of Lazarus."

I also laugh, embarrassed by my mistake. She offers me a glass of clear water. I see her hands are strong and steady, with long, slender fingers. I know she still does physical therapy with handicapped children at a local clinic. In the bright light of midday I also observe soup stains on her white blouse. At age seventy, her failing eyesight misses such details.

I politely inquire about her friend, Miss Kleintop, who also attended that farewell luncheon in Teheran.

"She's still in Hong Kong. You know we first met in Lebanon in 1945."

"I didn't know that."

"In those days we could drive from Beirut to Jerusalem. There were no borders."

"Does Miss Kleintop plan to come back to the Middle East?"

"Oh yes, she loves it here. Hong Kong has been a difficult mission. The people in the church she oversees speak Chinese."

"I see."

"She plans to come visit me next summer. But let's talk about you. What are you doing in Jerusalem?"

She's a gracious listener, so I tell her how I came to Israel and found work at the Baby Home. I don't need to tell her how much it means to me to be back in the Middle East and that much closer to my sons. Then I tell her about Benny's muscle weakness.

"Bring him out here, dear. Let me examine the little fellow."

I breathe a sigh of relief. That's what I came to hear.

The following Saturday, I ask for and get permission to take Benny out for the day. Nurse Aliza is pleased that I am taking a personal interest in the Arab orphan. I don't tell her my destination is in the West Bank. I know she would consider it dangerous to visit an Arab village. In my relatively short time in Israel, I've observed that Jews never ride on an Arab-owned bus. However, I notice that Arab workmen feel comfortable on Egged, the Jewish-owned bus service. As an American, I believe I'm neutral and therefore safe from physical attack (shaky logic). I also rationalize that FATAH will not plant bombs on their own bus systems (sound logic).

On the Arab bus, with curly-headed Benny in my arms, I get smiles and nods of approval from fellow passengers. They seem to recognize one of their own. Officially his ethnic origins have not been established. He is neither Jewish nor Muslim. The Rabbinate is carefully deliberating on this and, until they rule, Benny will remain uncircumcised. If the scant evidence available indicates that he is from a Jewish mother, he will be circumcised and adopted by a Jewish family. If they decide that his mother is an Arab, he will be placed for adoption with a Muslim family.

Benny clings to my neck for security. He has never been outside the Baby Home before. This is his first bus ride, his first contact with strangers, his first view of men. Safe in my arms, he clearly enjoys the outing. I feel his warm sweet breath on my skin as I hug him close.

In any case, he seldom cries, unless he is tired and needs a nap. Babies brought up in an institution learn there is no reward for crying. A concerned mother doesn't come rushing to meet their every need. It surprised and disturbed me to learn that only one night nurse is necessary for the entire floor. The babies are put to bed at 7:00 P.M. and they sleep without waking until the next morning. In contrast, I remember how Rodwin never slept an entire night through until he was two years old. I nursed Shadwin all night long in my bed.

We get off the bus in the middle of Bethany. Carrying Benny, I walk the short distance to Dr. Colby's villa. One of the children playing in the street sees me and runs to open the heavy gate. The neighborhood children love Dr. Colby because she gives them glasses of ice water anytime they ring her doorbell. In return, they run to open the gate when they see her car returning home. Now, I reap the rewards of her reputation in this village.

Dr. Colby's little office also serves as an examination room. Inside she runs her sensitive fingers up and down Benny's spine, tracing invisible nerves that only her trained hands can feel.

She turns to look at me. "It is probably poor blood circulation to the lower extremities. Manual massage will possibly bring back his strength."

A smile replaces my frown.

"I suggest you massage his back and legs twice a day." She demonstrates the technique.

Benny doesn't make a sound and seems to be enjoying the examination. When she is finished, I dress him in his flannel shirt and bibbed denim trousers. He sits contentedly in my lap as Dr. Colby and I have a cup of tea.

"Sharon, would you like to come to the Bible study I have in my home every Wednesday night?"

I hesitate. I don't want to tell her that I feel uneasy traveling alone in the West Bank after dark. I know there is a profound difference between Jewish men and Muslim men. In an Arab culture, any woman outside her home after dark is considered a prostitute and therefore fair game.

But I doubt Dr. Colby realizes this. She receives the dignity bestowed on age, and, as a doctor, she is treated with courtesy. Beside this, she is exceptionally revered and beloved in Bethany because she graciously receives everyone who knocks at her door. Some days it's the mayor, who lives in a mansion at the top of her street. Other days it's the mayor's drunken doorman looking to cadge a handout to buy alcohol. The ten children of the goat herder and his wife never fail to get a glass of ice water in the heat of summer. Though adjacent to Dr. Colby's villa, their home has neither electricity nor running water. The daughters still draw their water from the ancient town well.

"Can I bring my roommate Lesley? We do everything together."

Dr. Colby replies, "Of course, dear, we're a small group. Just the other believers who live in Bethany."

I try not to show my surprise that there are other Christians in Bethany. I thought she was the only one.

She walks me to the door as I shift Benny on to one hip and heft the knapsack with his diapers and bottle on the other. Before we say good-bye, Dr. Colby bows her head in a moment of prayer. No one leaves her house without this blessing, even Muslims and Jews.

The weeks and months fly by. My days are full at the WIZO Baby Home, and in the evenings there is always something going on in Jerusalem. Lesley and I could go to a church service or Bible study every night of the week if we chose to. Then there are concerts and plays, light shows, and pageants.

Massage and manipulation of Benny's legs seem to be paying off. Now, when I hold him by his fingers, his leg muscles stiffen as he tries to stand on tip-toe. Even though he has missed the stage of crawling, I know it won't be long before he is taking his first steps. Nurse Aliza is pleased with his progress, although I see something in her eyes that makes me fear for his future. I can't place that look, but it saddens and scares me. I am apprehensive about what she isn't saying, but I figure in time she will tell me what is bothering her.

The student nurses see how much I care for Benny and that is affecting their behavior. They now speak to him as kindly as they do the other children. It amazes them that Benny understands what I say to him in English.

Lesley's mother sent her a packet of Winnie the Pooh posters. I tacked a poster with Christopher Robin on the wall above Benny's bed.

"Where is Christopher Robin?" I ask Benny, excitement in my voice.

He pulls himself up by the bed rail and wobbling, points to the sturdy little boy in the poster. The student nurses are impressed with his progress both in speaking English and in standing.

I know from experience that toddlers can assimilate as many languages as they are exposed to. I had spoken English to Shadi, while his father, brother, and the servant spoke to him in Farsi. Once, standing in the aisle on a crowded bus in Teheran, he had begged me to get us a seat. "Sit, sit," he wailed in English.

I whispered in his ear, "Say it in Farsi." I had hoped a sitting passenger would understand and yield his seat to us.

Wednesday nights, Lesley and I attend the Bible study in Dr. Colby's home. We're getting to know the other Christians in Bethany. There are two brothers, Benjamin and Reuben, originally from New York. They call themselves Messianic Jews. This is a new concept to me—Jews who accept Jesus as Messiah. They rent an apartment from Abrahim, the man who owns the gift shop beside Lazarus' tomb. Abrahim is a Muslim and not likely to convert. He attends the Bible study to keep in touch with what the English-speaking people on his lane are doing. Shmuel, also a Messianic Jew from New York, lives with the two brothers.

Birgitta, a Swedish artist, runs a foster home for Arab children. I envy her, though I try not to show it. She had married an Iranian, like I did, but her husband let her take her daughter when he divorced her. Pearl is ten years old, about the same age as Rodwin. Like him, she has dark brown hair and a winsome smile. I daydream about Pearl growing up and marrying Rodwin. We would all live happily together in Bethany.

I also envy Birgitta because she is beautiful and talented. Her paintings are reproduced on calendars and cards, and Swedish tourists visit her little home in Bethany.

She is aware of her beauty and tries to minimize it by wearing plain navy smocks that reach her ankles. In my eyes, the navy serge and leather clogs look trendy. She covers her long platinum hair with a white gauzy scarf, but the tips of her bright hair are visible.

Sometimes, Benjamin and Reuben invite me to come out to Bethany for a hike in the hills. By mid-March the Judean desert is like a canvas painted with vivid acrylic colors. Red-orange anemone spread like marmalade between the white stones. Luscious purple lupine mass in regiments, standing erect and tall. White and fuchsia cyclamen seep out of the cracks in broken boulders.

As we leisurely walk the goat paths, Reuben points out garnet-colored flowers called the *Blood of Judas*. They do look like drops of blood. I pick some with long stems, which I will later hang upside down to dry, making a bouquet that will never wilt.

We sit on the green grass that covers the contours of the hills like fuzz on a ripe peach. The grass will be eaten by flocks of sheep and goats before the summer sun has a chance to scorch it off.

I find myself attracted to these two brothers, and not only because they share my faith. Reuben has black hair and green eyes. His strong nose is balanced by sensual but finely shaped lips. Benjamin is the older but shorter of the two. His hair is brown and his features regular, but he is not as dramatically handsome. He studied architecture but now devotes his time to creating artwork with a religious theme. He is quiet but the more dominant of the two. In conversation, Reuben yields to Benjamin.

I feel honored that the brothers one day reveal their secret chapel to me. They live in a one-bedroom apartment above Abrahim's home. Benjamin has transformed the only bedroom into a religious art form that I have never seen before. Every inch of the four walls is covered with murals depicting scenes from the Bible. The ceiling is dark blue with silver stars hanging from invisible strings. There is a handmade altar designed in what I'm guessing is the Byzantine style. The floor is covered with tribal carpets. In one corner is a life size creche and a Baby Jesus made out of porcelain. In another corner is a crucifix. Next to it hangs a painting of Jesus being taken down from the cross by Joseph of Arimathaea. The largest painting in the room shows three men, with halos around their heads, sitting at a table.

"What's that painting about?" I point to the one in question.

"Technically it's not a painting. It's been done with tiny strips of colored paper, ingeniously cut and pasted. It has taken Benjamin years of work," Reuben explains.

"Those three angels represent the trinity," Benjamin answers. "You remember the story in Genesis. Three men visit Abraham in the plain of Mamre. The Bible calls one of them the Angel of the Lord."

I am still standing in the doorway. Never in a million years did I expect two Jews born in New York to have created such a room. Reuben motions me to sit down. I look and see three little stools in front of a side altar.

"We've never shown this room to anyone."

I'm stunned more than flattered. I don't begin to know what it represents to them. I know their parents escaped the Nazis, but their grandparents did not. They were raised as orthodox Jews. Studying architecture in Denmark, Benjamin had a vision that revealed Jesus as the Messiah. He went to a Danish Church but felt no peace and has never had anything to do with organized Christianity since.

Reuben was living in a commune in Hawaii when his brother came and told him about his new faith in Jesus. The younger brother believed at once, and the two moved to Israel. They didn't fit in among the Jews so they moved to the West Bank and rented an apartment from Abrahim.

"We will never marry," Reuben tells me without preamble.

"What?" I respond as if I didn't hear what he said.

"We will devote our lives to God," Benjamin replies. "Shmuel has also taken the same vow."

"I've never heard of such a thing outside the Catholic church," I weakly reply.

"What's with these guys? I ask Lesley that night. "They want to be like monks." I say nothing about the hidden chapel, as I promised them.

"They're so handsome, what a waste," Lesley responds.

"We've got to respect their resolve," I say with a sigh.

I daydream about remarrying. I'm not lonely, but I miss having a sexual partner. I'm still young and would like to have more children. Some day I'll meet someone. Or maybe not. Perhaps I, like Birgitta, will live in a villa in Bethany with my sons, taking care of orphans.

Nurse Aliza calls me into her office the first day of the week. "Close the door, Sharona, I have something to tell you."

I sit stiffly in the chair opposite her cluttered desk. I have been waiting for the figurative "other shoe to fall." I know something is wrong. Other children Benny's age are quickly adopted or placed in foster homes. Every time a child from our floor is adopted, I run down the back stairs and hide behind the shrubs near the entrance, so I can check out the new parents. Adoptive parents are not allowed to meet the nurses because, in many cases, we know the birth mother. It's a joy to see the head administrator hand over a baby. The baby may have psoriasis, or a runny nose, yet the new parents hold him as if he is a bundle of pure gold.

"Simira's mother is here and wants to take her daughter back to Tel Aviv."

I'm relieved that this meeting is not about Benny.

"Simira's mother is a prostitute," Aliza continues.

I knew that. Nothing stays private for long among the nurses, but I say nothing.

"We can't allow her custody, but we have agreed that she can take her out for the day."

"Now?" I mentally decide to dress her in her prettiest outfit.

Simira's mother is short, chubby, and decidedly not beautiful. She is wearing a tight fitting sweater and clingy, black trousers. She swings her daughter out of the crib and covers her face and neck with kisses. Simira revels in the attention. I pack a bag with extra diapers and snacks and ruefully watch them leave.

When Simira is not back in time for supper, Aliza calls the police and they set up a search in Tel Aviv. I'm sick with worry. Will Simira's mother notice that she can eat only tiny portions of food at a time? I once came in on my day off and found a nurse shoving big spoonfuls into her already full mouth, causing her to choke. Then I had to show the nurse how to fill the tip of the spoon and give her plenty of time to swallow. How will her mother do? And who will take care of Simira while her mother is working? I've overheard the student nurses talking about Simira's mother. *Her "customers" must be Arabs. Why else would she give her daughter a decidedly Arabic name?* I can't bear to think of the outcome of such neglect.

I fretted in vain. One month later, Simira's mother voluntarily shows up at the Baby Home with a tanned, fat, and obviously happy little girl.

"Keep her until I can arrange my life," she says, then leaves.

Simira bawls for a week. I, too, cry for both mother and daughter.

One day without warning, Nurse Aliza informs me that Benny's blood tests have shown positive markers for syphilis.

"More tests have to be done."

"What does it mean?" I don't know enough to be alarmed.

"Children born with this disease seldom live more than five years."

"There will be no adoption for Benny?" As the implications seep in I feel a dull ache in my chest.

"I'm afraid not." She looks out the window to the treetops as if help might come from that direction. "His end will not be pleasant."

Unwilling to accept this grim prognosis I mentally scramble for answers. "There must be a drug that can cure him."

"The doctors at Hadassah Hospital know very little about in vitro syphilis. It's a rare disease in this country. A research assistant from America is going to do further tests on his blood in the coming weeks."

I can't sit by and do nothing. That evening, I skip supper and take a bus to Jaffa Gate. If I hurry, I will get to Gideon's Bible shop before it closes.

"Benny might die before he is five," I sob to Gideon. "He will die a slow horrible death."

"You are forgetting one thing, Sharona. Prayer."

We pray in the dusty little room, my tears spilling on a book or two. Gideon clumsily pats my shoulder. As the shadows darken in the street outside we concoct a plan to spirit Benny out of the country and take him to England or America where he can get more advanced treatment.

Later that night, I tell Lesley the whole story. She spontaneously offers her mother's house in Kent. Mentally making plans, no matter how farfetched, is better than accepting the status quo.

The next day I tell Nurse Aliza that if nothing can be done for Benny in Israel, I will take him to England or America.

"I promise I will put no roadblocks in your way," she responds.

I take her comment to mean that she will give me a head start before reporting Benny as missing.

Two weeks later, the news comes back from Hadassah Hospital. Benny does not have syphilis. His blood tests show that his mother had the disease and only passed on the antibodies. I jump up and down with relief, then run and pick up Benny. We dance around the verandah while the other children laugh with glee, as if they understand that a death sentence has been commuted from one of their own.

Now his case worker can actively start an adoption file. The Rabbinate had already decided that he was Jewish. I assume this is based on the fact that he was found in a Jewish town with almost no Muslim population. I have mixed feelings about his adoption.

I love him, but I don't earn enough to raise a child on my own. So on one hand, I'm relieved that he will have a mother and father and a real home. On the other hand, it hurts to say good-bye to another child.

Summer turns into fall and preparations are being made for the Holy Spirit Conference to be held in Jerusalem. Jimi and Bob Old come from Teheran and stay with Dr. Colby. I'm eager to hear all the news about Rodwin and Shadwin.

"The boys are growing up, as you can see from these photographs," Jimi says as she hands me an envelope.

I gaze at them, one by one. Rodwin looks the same, just a little taller. He stands proudly with his hands at his sides, looking directly into the camera. But Shadwin has changed so much I hardly recognize him. His baby fat is gone, his once round face longer and angular. He is now a stranger to me. If I met him on the street would I even know him? I have missed crucial years in his development and, even worse, I recognize that my dream of regaining custody is just that. Only a dream.

Heavy sadness overwhelms and covers me like an invisible veil. I feel like the Muslim women in *purdah,* with their faces hidden. I exist only in my own head. I quietly slip the photos into my purse. I don't cry or show any emotion, but Dr. Colby hands me a cup of tea with great gentleness. She seems to intuit my state of mind.

During the next few weeks and months, Dr. Colby never once brings up the subject of my children. We make many day trips to Jericho to drink glasses of fresh squeezed orange juice. "It's for my emphysema," she says. "And, I can breathe better below sea level."

I know she is making these trips for my benefit. She has noticed that, at the Bible studies, I have quit making any contributions. Neither do I participate in the voluntary prayer. I'm not mad at God, just depressed. She seems to understand.

"I know what disappointment is. Thirty years ago in Lebanon," she tells me, "my husband left me for another woman. I haven't been able to physically shed tears since that day."

I hug her tight, our mutual sorrows binding us together in love.

My first year in Jerusalem has passed. It's spring again and a family from a religious kibbutz wants to adopt Benny. The social worker and Aliza have agreed that the process should move slowly because Benny is now bonded to me as if I were his mother.

In this situation, an exception is made to the rule that nurses and adoptive parents never meet. Benny's new father and mother will come visit him once a week to ease the transition. This also gives me time to gently break the tendrils of love that have grown between us.

Before Jimi and Bob return to Teheran, they relate the newest teaching that is sweeping Evangelical groups in America.

"It's called *covering*," says Jimi. "Every woman in the Body of Christ needs to be spiritually covered by her husband or by a minister if she is single. For her own protection."

I see from Dr. Colby's face that she is not impressed. *I've been on my own for the past fifty years and haven't done badly*, I read in her expression.

"What's this got to do with me?" I ask. What I'm thinking is women in the Middle East are certainly covered. From head to foot. Orthodox Jewish women cover their heads with both a wig and hat. What's so dangerous about hair? My hair is thick, wavy, and falls below my shoulders. I often twist it up and secure it with a barrette like secular Israeli women do. Short or long, no one pays much attention to hairstyle. All of a sudden I need spiritual covering? As protection from whom? What?

Obviously, Jimi has given this a lot of thought. That very week, she introduces me to an American couple living on Mt. Scopus. The husband is a minister on sabbatical. He and his wife agree to be my spiritual cover in lieu of a husband's covering. This whole concept of "covering" eludes me. I have Toots and Pete who look out for me as if I am their daughter, and that seems sufficient. But to please Jimi and Bob I go along with them.

Something positive develops out of this rather forced introduction to the Americans on Mount Scopus. A young woman from Rhodesia is living with them. Her name is Esther. She is petite, with auburn hair and eyes the color of a tranquil tropical sea. Her parents were born in Lithuania and fled to Africa one step ahead of the Nazis.

I introduce Esther to Lesley and the three of us are soon best of friends. Saturday we attend the worship service at the Baptist House on Narkis Street. Sunday mornings we go to the outdoor service at the Garden Tomb in East Jerusalem, never guessing that Esther would eventually marry the young pastor at the Garden Tomb.

The three of us hike the barren trails in the Judean wilderness. Hot and dusty, we dip our feet in the ancient pools that David and his band of warriors used when fleeing from King Saul. We catch glimpses of mountain goats scrambling up sheer precipices on tiny black hoofs. The elusive conies, the size and shape of large hamsters, stare at us as we pass their colony in rock piles near the trail.

I've been working at the Baby Home for more than a year and have some vacation time due. I decide to join a group from the Baptist House on a camping trip in the Sinai. Five people sign up, three men and two women. Gideon is one of the men, and the other female is an American tourist named Nola. Once again fate, or the hand of God as I prefer to call it, has placed someone in my life that will be pivotal. Nola and I will become closer than sisters, although we have no inkling of this at the time.

"This is our last chance to see Mount Sinai, before Israel gives it back to Egypt," Nola tells me.

"Israel gained this territory in bitterly fought battles. The Six Day War," Gideon adds.

"Nobody lives there except wandering tribes of Bedouin." I know that much.

This camping trip is to be done on the proverbial shoestring. To save money, we buy our food in Jerusalem, rather than let the tour company supply the food. We pack sleeping bags and food, and we all pile on the public bus that takes us from Jerusalem to Eilat in the Gulf of Aqaba. We pass hotels where tourists are wallowing in the healing mud baths of the Dead Sea. Then we see no signs of habitation for hundreds of miles. The desert here is bleak and uninviting.

"We've just passed through Sodom," Nola says reading a road sign from the bus window.

I look back over my shoulder and see nothing but ragged cliffs, sheer white in the blazing noon heat. "Wake me when we get to Eilat," I say and try to sleep. But the heat keeps me awake.

"Tell me about your life before Israel," I say to Nola just to pass the time.

"I grew up on a dairy farm. I played on rolls of baled hay instead of a jungle gym." Nola wistfully twists strands of red hair around her finger.

"Yeah? My dad loved to milk cows when he was young. His dream is to retire with one or two milk cows," I reply.

"I thought you grew up in Los Angeles?"

"I did. But my father was born in Missouri."

"When I wanted to come to Israel, I asked my parents to sell a cow."

"The price of one milk cow was enough?" I'm duly impressed. I also feel a warm surge of empathy with Nola because she appreciates cows like my dad does. I sense we are going to be good friends, not just chance travel companions.

We arrive in the port city of Eilat before the sun sets. It is still around 100 degrees.

"Follow me," Gideon says, taking command of our group. "I know a place we can camp for the night."

After arranging our sleeping bags under a grove of palm trees, Nola and I change into bathing suits and race down to the shore. The water is cool and refreshing after the long drive through the desert. Floating on my back, I can see the Jewish town of Eilat in one direction. Across the bay I see the lights of Aqaba on the Jordanian side.

"Watch out for sharks." Nola shouts over her shoulder. Swimming with strong strokes, she heads for the coral island off shore.

Nola grew up on a dairy farm in Wisconsin, but she is a far stronger swimmer than I am after growing up in Southern California. I try to catch up with her but soon tire. I see a fin out of the corner of my eye. Shark! My blood freezes. A feeble croak escapes my lips. Nola is too far ahead to hear my cries for help even if I were able to scream. Gideon and the others are setting up camp under the palm trees and can't hear me.

Holding my breath, and stiff with fear, I look back at the shark to gauge the distance between myself and death. The creature leaps out of the water. It's a dolphin! Tears of relief trickle out of the corners of my eyes as I slowly head back to shore. The dolphin follows me. I slow down, it slows down. I dog paddle in a holding pattern, and it stays with me. I turn over and backstroke a few yards. The dolphin mimics all my movements. I've found a friend who wants to play. But I'm tired, and the light is fading. I continue on to shore.

After so much excitement, I expect to sleep like a baby and dream of my aquatic friend. I don't. The constant rustling of the rats in the palm trees keeps me awake most of the night. The next morning, bleary with fatigue, we break camp and go to meet our tour guide.

Moshe is an ex-paratrooper who knows the dirt roads and trails of the Sinai from his time in military service. He says he has never before guided a group of tourists who insisted on bringing their own food to save money.

"I would have provided steak," he says, ruefully inspecting our boxes of peanut butter, bread, rice crispies, and canned milk.

I glare at Gideon as if to say I told you so. I emphatically did not want to eat peanut butter and rice crispies and had complained to no avail in Jerusalem.

Setting off from Eilat, we head into the interior of the Sinai desert. Moshe owns a four-wheel-drive jeep, which is necessary on the rutted, sandy tracks. Our destination is Santa Catarina, a Greek Orthodox Monastery nestled at the base of Mount Sinai. We arrive shortly before nightfall and pitch camp in the empty plain before the high mountain peak. The air is incredibly clear and sweet to our lungs. After our meager dinner of canned beans, with Moshe still murmuring about steak, we crawl into our sleeping bags and stare into a canopy of stars so bright we don't need flashlights.

I wake before dawn to the comforting smell of coffee. Moshe has already boiled the water and made a large pot of Turkish coffee. I crawl out of my sleeping bag, dressed in the clothes I slept in, and look for a bush. There is an acacia tree, but it is too scrawny to offer any privacy. I find a scraggly bush and do what is necessary. Back at the camp, the thick, sweet coffee tastes better than anything I have tasted before. The crisp morning air is invigorating.

Moshe ignores the rice crispies. He eats a pita with his coffee, then deftly packs all the gear back onto the jeep.

"Y'allah. Get moving if you want to be at the peak in time for sunrise." Moshe leads us along a trail seen only by his eyes.

"But I want to visit the monks," says Gideon.

"Afterward," Moshe replies. "You don't want to miss the sunrise."

The trail is steep and narrow. We hike single file behind a Bedouin guide hired by Moshe. Gideon and I bring up the tail. Halfway up the mountain, I'm falling behind, gasping for breath. Nola is hiking with strong strides right behind the guide. There is something about these farm girls, I mutter to myself.

"Grab hold of my belt," Gideon says. "I'll pull you behind me."

"Thanks," I reply. The trail is much steeper than anything I have ever climbed before. Plus it is still dark, and I can see only one foot in front of the other. I continue to hang on to Gideon's waist.

At the point when I think I can't take another step, we reach the summit. I find a boulder to sit on and look out over the wide expanse of mountain ranges below us. The sun bursts over the distant peaks in hues of purple, fuchsia, and delicate gold as far as the eye can see. I sit in awed silence at the magnitude of rugged wilderness. Mentally, I thank Moshe for getting us up here just as dawn lights up the earth.

I am too moved to speak, and I don't want to spoil the moment by breaking the silence. The stillness is a physical presence as strong as a hand on my shoulder. There is no chatter of birds, chirping of locusts, or even the slithering of a lizard on a rock. Silence as crystal clear as ice permeates the mountain peak surrounding us. I feel insignificant, less than a blade of grass.

The hike down the mountain is less taxing, but more precarious due to the loose gravel underfoot. Still, we make it in half the time it took to reach the summit. At the monastery gate, the Bedouin leaves us without so much as a glance over his shoulder. We enter the courtyard where we are met by a young man in a black robe and strange stovetop hat. He explains, in good English, that he is a novice at the monastery. It is his duty to show guests around the grounds and buildings. He never once smiles, and I deduce this is not his favorite task. After all, he chose to live in this isolated spot for its solitude.

We file into the small chapel that commemorates the burning bush where God first spoke to Moses. The air is musty with the sweet scent of incense. Brass lamps hang from every available hook. In the ornate Greek Orthodox style, icons, candles, tapestries, and carpets overwhelm my American sense of esthetics. It reminds me of the Church of the Nativity in Bethlehem. Or the Holy Sepulcher in Jerusalem.

"Way overdone," I whisper to Nola in a tone of superiority.

Our guide takes us through the now empty refectory where the monks eat at plain wooden tables. Then we go behind the main buildings to the charnel house to view the skulls of monks who have passed on.

"We view our own death as a thing to cherish and look forward to," the young monk intones. "The charnel house reminds us that all flesh is but grass that springs up, then withers away."

Rows and rows of skulls look down on us with their mirthless grins. I shudder and look away. I, too, look forward to Heaven, but here on earth I prefer not to anticipate death, especially my own.

I think I have nothing in common with these monks. It's not possible they follow the same Lord. I decide we aren't on the same pathway, never realizing how narrow my religious outlook is.

Moshe adeptly drives us down the mountains and into the desert plains, following faint wheel tracks of military jeeps. We keep traveling through the heat of day and only stop when someone has to relieve himself behind a rock. We continue on until the full moon is hanging over us, so near I pretend I can reach out and touch it.

We finally stop and make camp at a desert oasis. In the moonlight I can see the tents of Bedouin set up in the palm grove. Moshe tells us there is a hot spring here, and we can bathe if we want to. He nods to Nola and me, giving us first go at it.

I grab a bar of soap and some shampoo from out of my backpack and head over to the mineral springs. I can hardly wait to get out of my smelly tee shirt. Inside the slatted shelter built over the hot springs, I strip and slide into the steamy water. The stones are slimy to the touch, but I don't care. I need a bath. Nola and I sit in the hot water up to our necks, letting the heat relax our stiff muscles and melt away the dirt. Enough moonlight penetrates the enclosure to enable us to see if we have rinsed off all the suds. We dry ourselves, put on clean underwear, jeans, and shirts and go back to our sleeping bags. We fall asleep despite the shrieks and shouts of the guys horsing around in the baths.

Moshe lets us all sleep. The sun is hot on my cheek when I first stir. I sit up in my sleeping bag and stare at the unexpected activity all around our camp.

"Hey, Nola, wake up! You aren't going to believe this!"

Nola slowly turns over and raises her head. "What the heck!" She sits straight up when she realizes she is surrounded by jeeps and tanks. While we slept, an army unit had moved in and set up camp.

"Aren't you glad we took our bath last night?" I asked.

"You bet," she says grinning broadly.

After breakfast I wander over to the Bedouin's camp to take pictures of two little girls sitting on the outskirts. They smile and remove their veil when they see I'm alone. They look to be about eight years old, but I figure they are probably a few years older because their veils indicate they are betrothed. Wearing robes of tattered black cloth with no embroidery or adornment, they dance about on bare feet. When I raise my camera to take a picture, they reach up and pull the loose cloth across the lower half of their face. Large, black, expressive eyes look intently into my camera.

We pack the jeep and leave the oasis behind and head for Ras Mohammed at the point of the Sinai Peninsula.

"Best snorkeling in the world," Moshe boasts.

"We don't have snorkeling gear," Gideon protests.

"Not to worry," Moshe smiles. "I have thought of everything.

We arrive at the Red Sea in the early afternoon with plenty of time to swim and snorkel. Moshe warns us to keep our sneakers on to avoid cuts from the coral. The water is waist deep and calm. I put on a mask and, floating face down, enter another realm. I see tiger fish, butterfly fish, sea anemone, and coral in distinctive shapes ranging from mushrooms to moose antlers, cabbages, luted pillars, and wrinkled brains. Jellyfish pulse gently as they drift by. How could something so beautiful be made of such icky material?

Moshe warns us to stay away from the jellyfish called the Lion's Mane. The sting of its tentacles hurts but almost never kills. The moon jelly turns translucent before my eyes in an attempt to hide from what it thinks is a predator.

In the shallow water I almost step on what looks like an algae-covered rock, only to discover it is a frogfish. A sea worm, the size of a small carrot, emerges from the sandy bottom and spreads jaws that look like miniature ice tongs. A pink sea anemone the size of an open umbrella spreads itself over the sand. Little gold and black fish hover over it. A scorpion fish swims by and opens its mouth in a gigantic yawn.

These coral reefs reveal their treasures like jewels scattered by a benevolent and creative master. The water is the temperature of blood, and I feel completely at ease, like floating once again in my mother's womb.

Abruptly, I am looking down into an abyss hundreds of feet deep. The coral and rich sea life have disappeared. I have drifted out over the continental shelf and have the sensation of falling into a chasm as deep as the Grand Canyon. I know this is unreasonable, but the sensation persists. Quickly, I swim back to shallow water and feel relief when I put my feet on the sandy bottom. I pull off the mask and snorkel and suck in air as if I were a near drowning victim. I immediately sense that this experience is a metaphor for my life. I was always safe in the circle of my family. Then I eloped with Mansoor and fell into a bottomless chasm. Israel represents solid footing, where I am once again safe.

Back on the beach, I sit on the warm sand, grateful to be alive. The rest of the group is still in the water and pays no attention to me. I have no need of a towel; the hot air of the Sinai dries me instantly.

Seven

Another full year has passed. It is now late February, 1976, and the almond trees in Bethany blossom overnight. Dr. Colby's compound looks like a Japanese garden. Some trees have pure white flowers, others a delicate shell pink. Most trees will produce edible almonds. The tree by the kitchen window has gone bad and will produce bitter almonds, tasting faintly of strychnine.

It is also a bittersweet season for me. The WIZO Baby Home in Bet HaKarem has closed its doors. All the infants and children have been adopted, returned home, or placed in foster homes. This is good, I tell myself. As much as the nurses and aides love the children, it is still an institution with a change of staff every eight hours. The Department of Social Welfare has wisely decided that an institutional atmosphere is not the best place to raise babies, and I agree. Still it is difficult to say good-bye to the children and to my life there.

Benny is now living on a kibbutz with his new mother and father. They made the long drive up from the Negev every weekend to visit Benny until he got to know them. Then one day they arrived in a taxi to take Benny back with them. I was mentally prepared for this and knew it was the right thing. Yet when his new mother, handed me a bouquet of flowers as we stood in the driveway of the orphanage, I had many doubts.

Would he adapt to Hebrew? After all, I spoke only in English to him. Would he sleep in his parents' home or in a children's house? I had so many questions that could not be addressed because I was required to act like a professional nurse, not the child's mother. Could I stay in contact with the family? No, that had been established early on. His adoptive mother felt he would adapt better to his new life if he never heard from me again. I agreed, even though it was a painful decision.

Benny placed his little hand in his father's outstretched palm and walked to the waiting vehicle without a glance back. I brushed away a tear, at the same time marveling at his trust and devotion to his new father. There are no men in the lives of orphans. All the caregivers are women, yet these children are instinctively drawn to a father if they get the chance to have one.

With the family in the back seat, the driver started the engine and slowly moved down the gravel driveway. Benny leapt out of his mother's arms and turned to look out the back window. It only then dawned on him that I was not coming on this ride. His little features distorted in fear and alarm. My heart physically ached. I watched his mother pick him up and place him in his father's arms. I knew then that all would be well with him.

With the closing of the Baby Home, I now need a new job and a place to live. I don't have to search long. Dr. Colby needs someone to cook for her and her new houseguests.

Skip and Dorothy are in their seventies and have been studying Hebrew at a residential Ulpan in Netanya. Dorothy has been ill for some time (most likely cancer, but she refuses to go to the hospital for tests) and has come to Bethany to die in Dr. Colby's guest bedroom. She is still a beautiful woman, elegant in impeccably tailored silk blouses. Skip looks the way someone called Skip should look.

White hair, robust features, congenial, and upbeat. He stays by her side day and night. Their son and daughter come from the United States. Miss Kleintop has taken leave from her duties in Hong Kong to assist Dr. Colby with the extra driving and shopping. My task is to cook and serve three meals a day. Miss Kleintop gives me her family's recipe for potato soup. It calls for hard-boiled eggs, which makes it especially nourishing. I already know how to make various Persian rice dishes, in addition to my favorite American casseroles and stews. I sleep on a cot on the back sun porch as all the bedrooms are filled.

There is no time to miss my life at the Baby Home. The approaching death is all consuming for everyone in the household. Even though I'm somewhat emotionally detached because I didn't know Dorothy, the mystery of approaching death is palpable. Ironically, Dorothy has come to Bethany to die in a house directly across from the tomb of Lazarus, whom Jesus called to come out of the grave. There is to be no resurrection now, and no one expects there to be. Perhaps Skip, in his heart of hearts, hopes for such a miracle, but this is only speculation on my part as I observe his deep love and devotion to his wife of fifty years.

Dr. Colby employs a man from Gaza to do the heavy housework. Abrahim is in his forties, small and wiry. He picked up his English working for UN families in the area. He sweeps, mops the floors, beats the carpets, and washes the laundry by hand. The wet laundry is hung to dry on the flat rooftop.

When he irons the linen, he takes a mouthful of water and sprays it over the heavy wrinkles. He has two wives and twelve children living in Gaza. Every Friday he goes home for a three-day weekend. Dr. Colby pays him well in American dollars that he exchanges at a favorable rate. He never goes home without bundles of clothes that Dr. Colby has collected from other Americans living in Jerusalem.

"Sharona, look at this." Abrahim beckons me to view the array of saucers and bowls lined up on the tile floor of the kitchen.

"Fifteen bowls!" He shrugs and rolls his eyes as I count all the cat food dishes.

Dr. Colby has three cats that sleep on her bed, forming a furry blanket over her feet. She also has a little white Maltese dog she calls "Pooky" that sleeps next to her bed. She feeds all the animals herself, giving them the leftovers. Her cats are finicky eaters, however, and each one has two or three choices. The inside cats are spoiled pets and are treated with special care. The feral outside cats eat anything she puts out for them. Every night after dinner she shares her bounty with all the strays in Bethany.

When an abandoned dog comes by (and they all seem to know that there is a safe haven in Dr. Colby's garden) she feeds them until they are tame and docile. Then she finds a family, usually Americans, to adopt them. She has given several strays to her grocer in East Jerusalem. He has a farm in Jericho and says he can use any number of watchdogs. I don't have the heart to remind Dr. Colby that this Arab also makes and sells sausage in his shop.

As Dorothy grows weaker, a Dutch nurse called Dinnee comes every morning to tend to her needs. Dinnee is tall and strong with the ever cheerful demeanor typical of her countrymen. She is beautiful with dark hair, sparkling eyes, and capable hands. She works in a convalescent hospice in Bethany founded by a Greek woman named Madam Sik-sik. Dutch philanthropists fund the hospice and pay the salary of the nurses and doctors. Every week, Dr. Colby, Miss Kleintop, and I go to Madame Sik-sik's to visit the elderly, bedridden patients and the children with severe birth defects. In Muslim culture, the old and disabled are cared for at home by relatives. Among the poorest, though, that is not always possible.

"It won't be long now," Dinnee tells me one morning. "Dorothy will die today or tomorrow." We are sitting in the kitchen drinking coffee at the Formica table. Cinnamon buns are baking in the oven and fill the house with a lovely fragrance.

"How can you tell?" I ask. Privately I believe that Dinnee is a miracle worker and can do anything. I'm in awe of her indefatigable spirit. I always return from those weekly visits to Madame Sik-sik's with a heavy heart and have to take a nap.

"Her kidneys have shut down. It is only a matter of time."

I admire Dinnee's calm, practical manner. She, like me, is not grieving as are the members of Dorothy's family. I feel I should stay in the background. So I bake bread and cakes, braise pot roast, and chop vegetables. It is as Dinnee says it will be. Dorothy does not make it through the night. Skip never leaves his wife's side.

Shulamit, the director of the Ulpan, the Hebrew school in Netanya, is summoned to Bethany. She grew fond of Skip and Dorothy during the time they lived at her school. She arrives after midnight, driven by her chauffeur. She spends the night sitting at the foot of Dorothy's bed. Her driver waits in the solarium. I sit with him and together we drink hot, strong coffee. To pass the time, he tells me about Shulamit's renowned family. Her father was a member of the Knesset, or parliament, of the fledgling state, and her uncle was once President.

I stay on at Dr. Colby's home through the spring and summer. Shulamit offers me a job caring for her invalid father in Netanya, but I decline, feeling I would be overwhelmed and subsumed by a such a dynamic and powerful family. I'm still trying to come to terms with the direction that my life is taking. I don't know how to define myself anymore. I am no longer a wife, mother, or baby nurse. I feel my personality will be extinguished altogether if I take on the task of caregiver in such a powerful family. So I wait in Bethany for another door of opportunity to open.

Dr. Colby doesn't sleep well, only falling asleep near dawn, so she often gets up late in the morning. Then it is her custom to share the Lord's Supper every day. We sit in the wicker chairs in the solarium and drink grape juice and eat broken matzo. Afterwards, we have pancakes, eggs, and coffee that I have prepared.

We go about our various duties during the day and play Scrabble every evening after supper. Dr. Colby and Miss Kleintop have known each other for more than fifty years and are comfortable and content in the house in Bethany. As for me, I'm growing increasingly restless and eager to move on with my life.

I'm still in contact with my sons. I write to Rodwin and he writes back. But Shadwin hardly remembers me. I force myself to put that part of my life on hold, knowing there is nothing that can be done. It is still a small comfort to know that I am in the Middle East and could fly to Teheran in a matter of hours if necessary. I often go up on the rooftop to be alone. I can see the spires of churches and the minarets of mosques. The aroma of goat meat roasting over charcoal drifts by me. I pretend that I want to watch the sunset, but it is really to hide my increasing depression that I stay there so long.

The ebb and flow of the village life in Bethany swirls around us (the Americans) without touching us. Occasionally Dr. Colby is called upon to help out in a difficult situation. Her neighbor, the goatherder's wife and mother of ten, knocks on the door one warm summer evening. She refuses to sit in a chair, but stands near the door. She is dressed in the traditional white tunic with a scarf covering her hair. She weeps and wrings her hands as her middle son translates for her.

"Doktora, you must help my daughter," the mother pleads.

"Of course, dear, what can I do to help? Dr. Colby responds.

"The police have her in custody, but I am afraid that her father or brothers may kill her."

Dr. Colby turns with a look of alarm to her friend Hazel. They have lived in Muslim countries long enough to know that a young woman's life is not worth much if she has betrayed the family's honor.

"What has she done?" Dr. Colby asks even as she knows what the answer will be.

"Tomorrow was to be her wedding day. We betrothed her to a cousin in Ramallah," the mother replies, wiping her tears on the sleeve of her gown.

I'm standing off to the side but listening intently to this drama play out. I have often seen this daughter drawing water from the village well. They are one of the few families in Bethany without plumbing or electricity, even though they own their own home and a large herd of valuable goats.

I think Zamira is stunningly beautiful, and I'm sure the groom's family paid plenty to win her hand for their son, even if her father is a goat herder. Her hair is black and she has violet eyes surrounded by thick lashes. In any Western country, she would likely win beauty contests and go on to be an actress.

The mother continues her lament. "Zamira ran off the night before her wedding with her uncle. They were found hiding in his hometown and the police have taken her into custody. For her own protection they say."

"What can I do?" asks Dr. Colby.

I wonder how the uncle got involved. Did Zamira fall in love with him? Or he with her? Did he seduce her? Why isn't he in trouble? I keep my questions to myself.

"Come reason with her father and brothers. They will try to strangle her, the first chance they get."

With Miss Kleintop driving, Dr. Colby rushes to the police station. I stay home and wait for their return. Many hours later, ill with exhaustion, they return.

I place a tureen of hot soup on the kitchen table and slice a loaf of bread. While they eat, Miss Kleintop fills me in.

"Zamira is still a virgin, and the young groom has agreed to marry her despite everything that's happened. Tomorrow, his family will take her from the police station to their home. It will be a quiet wedding, foregoing the big feast."

I feel immediate relief and think, all's well that ends well. But Dr. Colby intuits that it will not go well for Zamira.

"We may have saved her from an early demise, but the rest of her life will not be easy. I doubt they will let that girl out of the house for a long time," Dr. Colby says in a voice tinged with resignation. It is now after midnight and we go to our beds, each of us silent in our own thoughts.

Her words are accurate. It is a year before the new bride is allowed to leave her in-laws' home even to go to the market. She never again returns to visit her mother and siblings in Bethany.

Before I left the Baby Home, Aliza the Head Nurse suggested that I had an aptitude for nursing and I should consider nursing school at Hadassah Hospital. The idea appealed to me (I considered a career in nursing when I was a senior in high school), but first I need to speak, read, and write Hebrew. For this purpose, I enroll in a Hebrew Ulpan.

After two years in Israel I'm forced to admit that I'm not one of those people who pick up new languages by osmosis. I have to see it written on paper and in my mind's eye before I can pronounce it. It was different in Iran.

There I was surrounded by Mansoor's family, servants and shopkeepers who didn't speak any English. Therefore, I was forced to learn a minimum of Farsi.

In Israel, English speakers can exist nicely without knowing the local language. Even in Bethany, where the language is Arabic, I get by with only English.

I enroll in a class, commuting daily from the West Bank to central Jerusalem to attend Hebrew classes. I have already taught myself the Hebrew alphabet. Out of necessity, I have learned to pronounce the difficult names of local streets and cities. Now, I will learn to actually carry on a conversation.

The Ulpan is free to all new immigrants. Visitors like myself pay only a nominal fee. By necessity, Hebrew is taught in Hebrew in a language immersion program. There is no common language in the classroom. My fellow students are from Russia, Romania, France, South America, Iran, Morocco, and India. New immigrants have six months to a year to learn the rudiments of Hebrew before they are obliged to find a job and become self supporting.

"*Boker tov*," the teacher says.

"*Boker or*," a few students answer. I am silent, not understanding a word being said.

Somehow this language immersion principle works. After a few weeks of total bewilderment, I pick up about a fourth of what the teacher is saying. Others are faster, and some as slow as I am. We all learn how to say our own name and where we are originally from and phrases like: How are you? What's new? What's the price of this? How do I get there? Stop the bus now!

When the teacher gets to basic principles of grammar, I'm totally lost. Everything she says goes right over my head. When she asks the class questions, a young woman from Romania is quick to raise her hand and answer in near-perfect Hebrew. The teacher makes the mistake of believing we are all at this young woman's level of understanding.

This makes me frustrated and angry, so at the coffee break I speak to the Romanian (in English of course).

"Why are you in this class? You already know Hebrew."

She laughs, which irritates me further.

"I'm here to encourage my father. He knows no Hebrew and he's quite shy."

"I can see that," I reply.

Her English is as good as her Hebrew, I grudgingly admit. The old, white-haired man sitting next to her in class never opens his mouth. Neither do I. Yet, we both persevere. At least we show up every day.

The Ulpan ends after three months. We pose on the front steps for our class photograph, smiling with pride and relief that this first session is over (I still treasure this photograph). There are no grades and nobody fails. You simply go on to the next level or repeat the class if you want to. I definitely have to repeat level one. The second time around I'm not so out of it. I actually understand what the teacher is saying when she introduces herself and says good morning. Now, I'm getting the hang of it. I repeat this basic Hebrew class and then I am ready to advance to the next level, which is reading and writing.

Hebrew is written from right to left, and there is little or no punctuation. However, the stumbling block for me is the system of vowels and consonants. To my dismay, I find modern Hebrew (as opposed to Biblical Hebrew) is written without vowels. There is just a string of consonants with implied vowels.

For beginners, the actual vowel symbols (a series of dashes and dots similar to Morse code) are included in the text, but I must have been absent from class or daydreaming when the teacher explained how to read and pronounce these vowel sounds. I don't know enough to realize that I have missed something vital. I just think that I'm rather thick and will never be good in Hebrew. Nevertheless, I continue taking classes for another three months.

With more optimism than is warranted, the day comes when I arrange to take the language proficiency exam at Hadassah Nursing School. The exam is given in a semi-circular study hall with rows and rows of desks. When I come in, the Proctor asks me a question in Hebrew. I reply in English. Then she hands me the test, turning to a colleague and saying in Hebrew, "And she thinks she can pass?"

I'll show her. I understand a lot more than I am able to express. I sit at a desk and take out a pencil. I look up at the clock on the wall. I can have all the time I need. The room is about half full, all of them new immigrants, as native-born Israelis do not have to take this language proficiency exam.

The room is silent. The only sound is the scratching of pencils on paper. I carefully try to read the top page, which is evidently a set of instructions on how to take the test. My mind is blank. I can't decipher one word. I have never seen or heard these words before. I can't even make an educated guess.

Waves of humiliation crash over my head. I feel light-headed as though I might faint. I sit frozen for several minutes that seem like hours. I have no choice. I turn in the blank exam to the Proctor and manage to walk steadily out of the study hall. I don't dare look up to see the smile that I know must be on her lips.

On the bus ride back to Bethany I berate myself. What was I thinking? How could I have imagined I was ready to take a serious course of study in a language I barely knew? The Golden Dome, the Mount of Olives, scenery that I normally enjoy, pass by in a blur of held back tears.

In Bethany, I'm grateful to find Dr. Colby and Miss Kleintop are not at home. The car is gone, so I know they have probably driven to Jericho for a glass of orange juice. I can't bear to face anyone, even though I know they will be kind.

I go to my bedroom and have a long cry. Disappointment is nothing new, yet its sharp edge hurts as much as always. Abrahim is washing laundry and stays discreetly out of my way when I emerge from my room. I go to Dr. Colby's study to call Aliza and tell her the news of my failure. I know she, more than anyone, hoped I would make it.

"Not to worry, Sharona. All you need is a little more study."

"You think so?"

I have my doubts. Can any amount of study help me?

"Go to a kibbutz for six months. There you will be surrounded with Hebrew speakers."

"Maybe you're right."

I see a flicker of light at the end of the tunnel. I live with Americans. All the Jews and Arabs I know speak English with me so that they can improve *their* language skills.

"Yes, I need a change of scenery. A place where everybody speaks Hebrew."

"Give it six months, Sharona, then take that exam again. New classes start every year."

As I hang up the phone I'm in a better frame of mind. Before Dr. Colby and Miss Kleintop return, I'm filled with excitement over my new plans. I even know which kibbutz I want to go to. I even know who my roommate will be. Nola! My red-haired friend from the Sinai trip is living on a kibbutz on the Carmel. She has written several times inviting me to join her. Now I will.

I make the necessary trip to the Kibbutz Movement Headquarters in Tel Aviv where they process all the volunteers. I'm older than most of the volunteers, who are just out of high school or college. Maybe this is why no one is surprised when I tell them which kibbutz I want, rather then having them make the choice. I fill out the paperwork and take a physical exam. Then I return to Bethany to pack my belongings.

"There is always a place for you here," Dr. Colby tells me as she hugs me tight.

"I'll return to Bethany every chance I get," I assure her. "Say good-bye to Benjamin and Reuben for me."

I would have gone over to their place to say farewell, but they are in Tel Aviv visiting their mother. I have already taken leave of Abrahim our neighbor, and Abrahim the house-cleaner.

This is a new beginning that I only partially understand. God called me to live in Jerusalem, back when I made that first unexpected visit after my expulsion from Iran. Now, I am going to be living in the north of the country. I would have more trepidation about leaving the Jerusalem area if I were not confident that I will be back in six months.

The kibbutz, or communal farm, sits high on the Carmel Mountain Range, east of the port city of Haifa and west of the Jezreel Valley. The Carmel has rich farmland interspersed with pine groves and a Druze village or two. The Druze, I am to learn, are indigenous people of Arab stock who follow their own mysterious religion, not Islam. Unlike the Palestinians, they live in peace with the Jews. I don't understand why it is this way with them. The Druze don't share their views with outsiders.

I settle into kibbutz life with enthusiasm and curiosity. It is the same energy I had at age eleven, when I went to a Girl Scout Camp in the San Jacinto Mountains overlooking Palm Springs. Here, Nola and I share a cabin with two metal beds, two lockers, and a sink. The communal shower and toilet facilities are outside.

The kibbutz system is organized on an egalitarian model. Everyone does manual labor, including the leaders. It might be field work, milk production or factory work. All take their turn washing dishes. In addition, each member receives housing, food, and a clothing allowance. They share equally in the profits (of course, not the volunteers, who only get free room and board).

On the first morning, the sound of nearby artillery fire catapults me out of my bed. Thinking war has started with the Syrians (thoughts of the 1973 attack during Yom Kippur are still fresh in my mind), I run to the door expecting to see tanks moving across the tidy green lawns. I observe a dairy worker in his rubber boots, leisurely heading to the cow barns. He is not running for cover. I turn to Nola, who is burrowed under her blanket with only a red ponytail showing.

"What's going on?" I'm nearly hysterical but trying to act calm. My voice betrays me.

Nola sits up and yawns. "The army stages mock battles in the fields adjoining us. You'll get used to it." She throws off her covers, revealing a creamy white figure that rivals a Botticelli painting.

The picking crew meets at the dining hall, where a team leader then drives us out to the orchards. I carry a gunny sack with a long handle slung over my shoulder. When the sack is filled, I empty it into a large bin and start over.

The work reminds me of an old Judy Garland musical with Mickey Rooney. They sang and danced as they picked California oranges. Here, the air is fresh, the sun is shining. Dressed in our navy shorts and shirts, the kibbutz uniform, we almost whistle as we work.

At 7:00 A.M., we stop to eat a breakfast of brown bread, chocolate spread, hard boiled eggs, tomatoes, and cucumbers, washed down with flasks of rich, dark coffee. By eight o'clock the sun beats on my bare head, sweat rolls down my back, and nasty thorns in the grapefruit trees scratch bloody trails on my skin. Each gunny sack feels heavier than the last. This is hard physical labor, not a Hollywood musical. By the third day, I wish that I had sewing skills like Nola. She spends her six hours mending torn sheets in the communal laundry room.

But I do have a skill, I remind myself. Thanks to my two years at the WIZO Baby Home, I am a trained *metapelet*, or caregiver. Children on a kibbutz don't sleep in the same house with their parents. They are divided into groups, according to age, and live in Children's Houses. The original kibbutz founders wanted a communal life where women were as free to work as the men. So they have metapelets care for their every need.

I am accepted to work in the Infants' House. I spend my mornings bathing, dressing, and feeding the babies under one year of age. Their mothers drop in to breast feed or play with them any time they have a spare moment, which is often. It is completely different from an orphanage. These children are loved and spoiled by parents, siblings, and even grandparents. For this reason, I do my job without emotional ties. There's no little neglected "Benny."

Even though I'm studying Hebrew every afternoon in a formal class setting, I feel as if I'm spinning my wheels. Kibbutz life is too much like being at camp. My laundry is washed, ironed, and mended by others. My meals are prepared, served, and cleaned up by others. I get a small allowance to buy toothpaste, toiletries, and candy in the kibbutz store. This makes me feel even more like a child.

Some of the American volunteers smuggle in hashish to break the monotony. Nola and I are not inclined to this form of recreation. Neither do we indulge in casual sex to while away our excessive amounts of free time. There is a small group of Christians who hold a weekly Bible study. Nola and I don't fit in with them, either. These Christians are unfailingly cheerful as they go about their duties. They want to "set a good example" and have reproved Nola and me for our many bouts of depression and endless crying jags.

I'm depressed, and with good reason, I tell myself. I have accepted but not embraced the circumstances that continue to separate me from Rodwin and Shadwin. Being surrounded by happy kibbutz families only makes it more painful. I can't seem to stop tears from flowing every time I'm alone in my cabin.

Nola's tears irritate the Christians even more than mine. I try to hide my tears. She cries non-stop in the dining room or at work. The sheets she mends are soaked with her tears.

"Don't be so sad, dear. You'll find a husband."

"There is a lid for every pot." The gray-haired ladies encourage Nola, even as they privately worry about the sparse number of eligible Christian men in a Jewish nation. They fear she has turned thirty with no prospects in sight.

The Christian contingent comes to our room one afternoon to give us an ultimatum.

"Nola and Sharon," the self-appointed leader says, "You are bad witnesses."

We stop sniffling and blow our noses in unison. We can't believe what we're hearing.

"Shape up or ship out."

We choose to ignore this rude bit of advice. The kibbutzniks don't take our sad-sack demeanor as a sign of failure. After all, this is Israel, just thirty years after World War II. One third of the population qualify as "walking wounded," with emotional wounds far greater than anything Nola and I have to cry about.

There are always reminders of this. One Friday evening it is my turn to work in the kitchen. The serving crew eat together in the back before the others sit down in the dining room.

"Thank God, we're alone this Sabbath. No goyim among us, " says the head cook.

His wife nudges him with her elbow and raises her eyebrows in my direction. He has forgotten, or doesn't know, that I am not a Jew.

I don't take it personally. I'm familiar with his story, just as everybody's story is common knowledge in such a small community. I know that his first family, wife and children, had been murdered by the goyim in Holland.

There isn't any place in Israel where one does not encounter these wounded souls. At the Baby Home in Jerusalem, there had been a cafeteria worker who stood over the serving line and glared at the students and staff, defying them to take a helping of schnitzel and rice.

"I feel as though she hates me and doesn't want me to eat," I told a student nurse.

"It's not you, Sharona. Her mind has been affected by the years of starvation in a concentration camp. She loves to prepare huge quantities of food, but she can't stand to see it consumed."

Then there was Joel. Before I started working at the Baby Home, I had a brief stint as a driver for a Bible Society. I drove a van filled with Bibles that Joel, an elderly German Jew, delivered to kibbutzim. He was middle-aged, balding, and he always wore a baggy, brown suit shiny with age. He spoke five languages in addition to Hebrew.

When Joel and I drove into a kibbutz, he would ask for the librarian. Joel would then offer her Bibles in any languages she wanted. The librarian always took a carton or two, then invited us to have a meal in the dining room.

Sometimes, we were not at a kibbutz at mealtime. As the day wore on, I would became increasingly hungry and wait for Joel to suggest we stop at a roadside cafe. He never did. Many times we returned to Jerusalem, not having eaten all day.

"I can't drive a truck all day and not eat," I complained one day at the Bible Society.

"We forgot to warn you that Joel has a food phobia. He suffered in the camps, you know. He can only eat when invited to. Even then it takes several strong invitations."

"What do I do?" I now understood the problem, but didn't have a solution.

"Always take a picnic basket of bread and cheese. Then, if there is no cafe available, you ask Joel to stop along the road. You take the food out, arrange it on a cloth, and invite him to eat. You start, he'll eventually join you."

In comparison, the excess baggage that Nola and I carry is inconsequential. A failed marriage or a nonexistent marriage is small stuff. Only to the American Christians does it matter that we are not always cheerful and optimistic. The kibbutzniks accept us, teary eyes and all. That is not to say that the Israelis pay much attention to any of us. Volunteers are a transient population that come and go every few months. The heart of the communal life is not affected by us in the least.

This bothers me. I always feel as if I'm on the outside looking in, not really comfortable with the volunteers and definitely not one of the permanent members. Because I have not yet found my place, when our Hebrew course winds up, I suggest to Nola that we move down the road to another kibbutz that is beginning a new study program.

On the second kibbutz, some things are the same. We share a rustic cabin, put in six hours of manual work, and attend classes in the afternoon. But instead of dealing with uptight Evangelicals who disapprove of us, we encounter a different misconception. Because Nola and I don't smoke hashish, drink beer, or mess around in our free time, the other volunteers come to the conclusion that we are Catholic nuns incognito.

"Come on, tell us the truth. You're working for the Vatican." This from a hippie from California who is not afraid to broach the issue.

"That's why the work supervisor is so polite to you." His girlfriend sounds almost envious.

Nola and I look at each other and laugh. It is true. Our supervisor stands ten feet from our cabin and gently calls, "Nola! Sharona! Time to get up!"

He barges into their rooms, routing them out of bed with, "Get up, you drunken bums!"

We try to assure them that we are not nuns. "Wouldn't we have to cover our hair?" I ask. We can't convince them.

Nola and I decide that it is not such a bad thing to be perceived as nuns. If we are treated unfairly, we can complain to the Pope and start a nasty incident between Israel and the Vatican. What power we have! We will always get the best work assignments.

It's not all work. The kibbutz takes us on a field trip (just like camp again) to the ski slopes on Mount Hermon. Of course, none of us has skis, so we improvise sleds out of sheets of plastic.

I hurtle down the beginners' slope, sitting on my butt with my knees drawn up to my chin. I pick up speed on the slick ice and whirl around facing the wrong direction. In this position I hit a fence post. Stunned, with the air knocked out of my lungs, I lie in the snow. I feel foolish and hope no one is looking. Then I panic because I can't get up. My legs won't move.

Because we are in a military zone with the Syrian border just a few miles away, there is a first-aid station manned by the Israeli Army. Medics pick me up and carry me on a stretcher to the doctor on duty.

"Try to bring your knees up to your chest."

I comply.

"You're fine. No spinal damage. Next?" He curtly dismisses me.

Nola helps me limp back to the waiting bus. I sit there until everyone is ready to leave. It is late at night before we get back to the kibbutz. By this time, I'm freezing and stiff from the pain in my lower back.

The kibbutz nurse meets the bus and helps me to my cabin. "Take off your wet trousers. I'll make you a cup of tea."

I continue to sit on the edge of the bed, strangely peaceful, but not complying. The nurse boils water in the electric kettle. Then she notices that I haven't moved. Recognizing the symptoms of shock, she undresses me, tucks me under the blankets, and makes me drink a heavily sugared cup of hot tea.

"Keep an eye on her," she says to Nola. "I'm going to call an ambulance."

By the time the ambulance gets there, the heat and sugar have restored me.

"I feel fine," I say bravely. I don't want to be taken to the hospital in the nearby town.

The next morning, I can't move.

"Nola, help me sit up. It feels like I've torn something in my lower back." I know nothing is broken. Otherwise the army doctor would not have turned me away. But I'm badly bruised and know I won't be up and about for a long time.

At the end of the week, I still can barely walk, shuffling my feet without picking them up. Nola has to help me to the restroom. All I can do is pee. My lower intestines are on strike. Nola has to pull me up off the toilet.

I stay awake at night due to the pain. Then I sleep most of the day. Nola brings all my meals to the cabin. I take on the paranoid tendencies of the bedridden, falsely accusing her of neglecting me. At this point, I decide I want Dr. Colby's expert opinion. The kibbutz nurse says it is only a torn cartilage. I worry it might be something worse.

Dr. Colby and Miss Kleintop arrive at the kibbutz in the gold Peugeot, the one she calls "Goldie." They ask several people for directions to my cabin. This allows plenty of time for the kibbutzniks to observe the *Vatican doctor and her driver*, who have come to check on the injured nun. For some reason that I will never understand, Miss Kleintop chooses to wear a long blue skirt and tunic. I have never before seen her in anything but a mid-calf length dress. Today she is wearing navy blue from neck to ankle. As a Protestant, she never wears a crucifix, but now she is wearing an Egyptian eternity symbol on a long chain around her neck. It can be mistaken for a cross, and often is.

Dr. Colby skillfully manipulates my spinal cord. Her gentle fingers release the pinched nerve that is causing the trouble. Then, she and Miss Kleintop take their leave. Before the golden Peugeot is out the kibbutz gates, I'm walking, albeit slowly, by myself to the bathroom. My torn cartilage eventually heals and my friendship with Nola is restored. However, the nuns incognito theory is now firmly fixed in the kibbutz lore and gossip.

One day I open my mail to find an invitation to spend the following weekend with Reuben and Benjamin in their new home in upper Galilee. Gideon, my friend from the Bible book shop at Jaffa Gate, will also be there.

On Friday, I take the bus north to the Galilee. During the three hours en route, I reminisce about the brothers' surprise departure from Bethany. I had been there when their trouble began, and it is etched in my memory.

It started with Yassar, the young Arab man whom they befriended and took into their home. Yassar had a difficult childhood. His mother died when he was an infant. His father's new wife disliked him, showing preference to the children eventually born to her. By age twelve, Yassar had run away from home to live on the streets in Jerusalem. He peddled gum to tourists, washed car windows, and occasionally picked pockets. With little formal education, he nevertheless learned to speak Hebrew and even some English.

One day Reuben met him at a bus stop and spoke to him about the Messiah Yeshua. Yassar, now in his early twenties, responded with an intensity that was more than simple politeness. When Reuben learned Yassar was a homeless street person, he invited him to come to Bethany for a meal. Yassar stayed for a month. He tried to fit in with these Jews from New York. Yassar kept his unruly black hair trimmed, shaved every day, even copied their American manners in eating.

He also gave his full attention to the daily study of Scripture. Yet, all this did not bridge the enormous cultural gap. Plus, they had no extra bedroom. Yassar slept in the living room. If guests came over, dirty socks, blankets and pillows had to be whisked away. Finally, Benjamin told him he would have to find a place to live.

I happened to stop by that fateful day. No one answered my knock, so I pushed open the door and stuck my head in.

"Anybody home?" I called. I could hear a commotion coming from the back.

"Sharona, call the police!" Reuben's strained voice came from the bathroom.

I hesitated, then cautiously approached. Shmuel and Benjamin had Yassar pinned face down in the bathtub with his arms behind his back. Then I noticed the broken glass from the bathroom door and the splatter of blood on the walls and floor.

"Yassar locked himself in the bathroom and tried to kill himself," Benjamin said. "Shmuel smashed the door and overpowered him."

"He's stronger than all three of us," Reuben panted, out of breath from the exertion. Though in his late twenties and slender, Reuben was not muscular. The only exercise he got was walking to and from the bus stop.

I ran back to Dr. Colby's home and called the police station in Bethlehem, Bethany being too small to have its own police force. Then I ran back to the apartment to see if I could help. I think it was grief, not rage, that compelled Yassar to go on this rampage. Nevertheless, I could see he was dangerously out of control.

Deathly quiet greeted me when I entered the open front door. *Oh my God, Yassar has overpowered and killed them all.* I tiptoed silently to the bathroom braced for the worst. But I found them still sitting on Yassar in the bathtub.

When the Palestinian policemen entered the open apartment door, I pointed to the bathroom. Only then could I breath normally.

They dragged the bloody and bedraggled Yassar to the living room.

"*Ya' Allah*, Yassar, what are these Jews doing to you?" said a uniformed policeman.

"You know him by name?" I asked, amazement causing my voice to rise.

The policeman chuckled. "Yassar is often in and out of jail on petty charges."

They took him to the hospital to get his arms and wrists bandaged. At the same time, they arrested Benjamin, Reuben, and Shmuel for unauthorized residence in the West Bank. It turns out that Dr. Colby and I could live there because we were not Jewish. But no Israeli could reside over the Green Line without permission from the military governor.

Dr. Colby and I discussed how to get the brothers out of jail.

"We need a man to help," she said.

Her suggestion set me back for a moment. Then I concurred. We would get no respect in an Arab police station. I couldn't forget the police station in Teheran. The police lied to me and laughed at my distress. I also needed a man to wrest my exit visa from the reluctant officials.

"I'll call our good friend Nathan and ask him to go with me. You stay here by the phone." Dr. Colby picked up Nathan in Jerusalem and drove to the police station in Bethlehem. After a lengthy discussion, they allowed her to post bail. The police gave the brothers seven days to move out of the West Bank. If they did not comply, they would be charged with assault.

The brothers quickly forgave Yassar. But I didn't. When I next saw him on the streets in Jerusalem, I glared at him then looked away.

Now, I'm on my way to visit the brothers in their new home in Upper Galilee. I look forward to this visit for several reasons. One, my time is up on the kibbutz and I'm not proficient enough in Hebrew to try the nursing school again. Second, Nola has already written and asked her mother to sell a dairy cow for her return ticket home. I don't want to stay on the kibbutz alone. Maybe the brothers will have a suggestion about what I should do. I know they will pray with me about the next step.

When the bus arrives in Tiberias, I transfer to a local connection heading for the Lebanese border. On my right is the Sea of Galilee. At the northern end of the sea, which is really a lake, I see the Mount of Beatitudes, easily identifiable by the red-roofed church seen in every tourist brochure. Now, the driver loudly changes gear as the road ascends to higher altitudes. The air is cooler, too, not stifling hot and sticky as it is around the lake. This is farm country, and I see an occasional kibbutz in the distance.

The upper Galilee is a long, narrow finger on my map. To the right is the Golan and Syria. To the left, behind the low mountains, is Lebanon. According to the map, I could drive to Damascus in one hour. I daydream about having coffee in the Arab souks, then hunting for treasures in the bazaar. It is only a dream. The border is heavily guarded by troops on both sides, with UN forces stationed in between. I guess it will be thirty or forty years, at best, before tourists can cross that border.

I get off the bus at the edge of Rosh Pinna, the small village where the brothers live. It's a long walk up the hill to their rented house. I recognize it from their description. *Look for the blue door with gold trim. It will have Bet Emmanuel painted on the wall above the doorbell.* I open the gate and enter the garden. The air is heavy with perfume from the jasmine vines climbing the stone walls. I'm sweating from exertion and probably stink as I ring the door bell.

Reuben opens the door and takes my shoulder bag. "Sharona, *baruch h'ba*, welcome." His big smile says he is genuinely pleased to see me. Once again, I silently appraise his physical beauty. His black curly hair contrasts perfectly with emerald green eyes. He never seems to be aware of the effect his appearance has on others.

I enter a foyer with a high ceiling and cool tile floors. We turn right and go through a double door to the sitting room. Two tall narrow windows let in filtered sun and a bit of air. Reuben puts down my bag and tells me to make myself comfortable. I sit on the sofa, which is a simple cot covered neatly in a gray army blanket. The walls are covered with murals painted by Benjamin. The overall effect is artistic, even austere. I can find no female touch, such as curtains at the windows or fancy throw pillows.

"You will sleep tonight on one of the divans." Then he leaves to let the others know I have arrived.

Gideon comes in first, his shock of wavy white hair surrounding his ruddy face like a halo. "I was in the kitchen reading my Bible. The others are out back hoeing weeds in the vegetable garden."

I give him a big hug then we sit down opposite each other. "How big is the property?" I ask. I can't picture these city guys working a garden.

"It's three dunam. About two acres."

I laugh at the thought of Benjamin, Reuben, and Shmuel with hoes and rakes in their smooth hands. They are too intellectual for manual labor, or so I thought.

"Don't laugh Sharona. They also work at a local produce factory, sorting plums in season."

"Well, that tells me how they support themselves in the middle of nowhere."

"How are you doing on the kibbutz? How is Nola?"

Nola had fallen for Gideon during our Sinai expedition. He didn't encourage her, but neither did he discourage her. When no relationship developed, Nola's feelings were hurt. But I don't mention that now.

Just as I am about to answer, the brothers come in, greet me, and sit down. Shmuel follows with a pitcher of ice water and a tray of glasses. I gratefully drink one glass full and ask for another.

"How did you guys find this beautiful house? And why in this obscure village?"

"We have a distant cousin who lives up the lane," answers Benjamin, "in what's called the hippie colony. We spent a weekend with Rachel. She showed us around the village and we found this cottage for rent."

I glance at the high beamed ceiling, the flagstone floors, and guess the age of this farmhouse to be at least a hundred years.

"If your cousin Rachel lives in the so-called hippie neighborhood, what do you call this?" I indicate with my eyes my present surroundings.

Shmuel laughs a deep, abandoned belly laugh. His red beard shakes. "Here in mid-village we are neither farmers nor hippies."

The sun sets quickly because we are on the eastern slopes of a mountain range. It is the Sabbath, and I can smell the homey savor of chicken stew. At 6:00 P.M., we troop into the kitchen and sit on benches around a wooden table. Then we sing songs of worship in Hebrew and English. No one plays a musical instrument so it is a cappella. When the singing ends, Benjamin stands and gives the traditional blessing. Then they sing another Sabbath song that I have never heard before. The others have apparently sung it all their lives.

Two loaves of challah, the braided Sabbath bread, are passed around the table and everyone tears off a hunk. Reuben goes around the table filling our plates with chicken and vegetables. Everyone eats and talks with enthusiasm. No formal manners are observed. Shmuel sucks the marrow out of a chicken bone with enthusiasm. There are no napkins on the table. I know paper products are expensive and cloth napkins without a washing machine can be a burden. I delicately lick my fingers clean, then surreptitiously wipe them on my skirt. After the table is cleared, instant coffee is served in thick mugs accompanied by a plate of vanilla cookies.

"I'll bake a cake tomorrow," I announce to nods of approval. I feel like Snow White having dinner with the Seven Dwarfs. It's a pleasant sensation.

Saturday morning I glance out the window at the property next door. Masses of orange, red, and yellow nasturtiums bloom in an artfully arranged rock garden. There are shrubs with pink blossoms that I can't identify, plus myriad other flowers. They delight the eye. I wonder who planted and tends this English-style garden.

"I see you admiring Mary's garden."

I turn to face Reuben. "Like the nursery rhyme? *Mary, Mary, quite contrary, how does your garden grow?*"

"You'll like her Sharona. She's a believer, like us."

"Yes, it would be nice to have some female company with all these men around."

"Mary's husband Arieh is hostile about her new faith, by the way. She also has a baby daughter, Sarah."

"I'd like to meet her. I'd also like to see her garden."

That very afternoon Reuben introduces me to Mary. She is slender, with light brown hair and a fair complexion. She speaks with a British accent, so I know my assessment about her English garden is correct. We sit at the kitchen table drinking tea, and Mary tells me how she came to Israel.

"I got fed up with my studies. I needed a change, so I trekked alone across North Africa. By boat, donkey, camel. Eventually I landed in Israel."

Her delicate build and soft voice belie a certain toughness. I would never have guessed this woman had been so adventurous.

"I stayed on a kibbutz and fell in love with Arieh. He's also originally from England."

"What does he do for a living?" I can't image what an educated, English-speaking person would find to do in this rural and isolated area.

"He drives a tractor for a local farmer. We rent the cottage next door. We don't own it."

That answers my next question. I genuinely like Mary and adore her chubby toddler. We seem to bond instantly in one of those friendships that are destined to endure.

Later that evening, when I meet Arieh, I find him intense but not in an unpleasant way. Reuben had earlier told me that Arieh was not a believer, in fact was openly hostile sometimes. This evening, he is the perfect English gentleman. In appearance, he is the opposite of Mary. Tall, angular, dark hair, and swarthy complexion. A Heathcliff type, I imagine. A bit rough compared with Mary's restrained demeanor. She delicately stirs in her sugar without touching the sides of her teacup. Arieh, as well as the brothers, vigorously clang metal against china with audible results. I notice that I do the same.

I've also learned this weekend to substitute the word believer for Christian. The terms are interchangeable as far as I am concerned. But the latter name has too many bad connotations for Jews, such as pogrom, inquisition, holocaust. Then there is the problem of language. In modern Hebrew, a gentile Christian is called a Naztir, meaning follower of the Nazarene, although the direct translation of the word Christian is Messianic. Therefore, most Hebrew-speaking believers call themselves Messianics. It's all rather confusing, but I'll get used to it, I suppose.

Now that I am no longer a volunteer on the kibbutz I return to Bethany to live with Dr. Colby. The hot desert air hits my face like a blast furnace, reminding me of summers in Teheran. No one has air conditioning, and adding to my discomfort is the lack of fresh water, as the Municipal Water Authority in Jerusalem has temporarily cut off water to Bethany. I know it's not collective punishment, still this never happened when I lived in West Jerusalem. Limiting municipal services to the Arab population is a common occurrence. They gave us a few days' notice so that we could fill the holding tank on the roof. To conserve this now precious water for drinking and cooking, I take a bucket to draw rain water from the cistern in the garden. It's contaminated with dust and leaves, but sufficient to flush the toilet. Dr. Colby and I take sponge baths, or bird baths as she calls them. We've been in the Middle East long enough that this temporary deprivation doesn't disturb our peace of mind inordinately.

Most homes in the village have cisterns to collect the scant rainfall. Before 1967, when Jordan controlled the West Bank, there was no clean, piped water. Cisterns and well water were all they had. But the Palestinians forget this and curse the Israelis for making their lives more difficult.

Then a letter comes from the Galilee. As the proverb says, *as cold waters to a thirsty soul, so is good news from afar*. Arieh and Mary write that they are going to England for two months and would like me to house-sit for them.

"Go Sharon. You will find your stay in the Galilee of great spiritual value. Plus, it's cooler there." Dr. Colby's words will prove to be right on target. As always.

"I'll miss you and Miss Kleintop." I mean it. Yet I'm thrilled at the opportunity to be with people my own age again.

"We'll come visit you. It's a great excuse to get out of this heat."

My new home is a three-room cottage built of fieldstone. The sitting room opens onto the bedroom, which opens onto the kitchen, like the cars on a train. I faithfully water Mary's beautiful garden. I'm relieved that she no longer keeps chickens. She stopped raising them because of the nightly raids by a local mongoose.

I start each day at 5:00 A.M. with a cup of coffee and then read my Bible. Breakfast is a cup of yogurt and a slice of brown bread spread with my favorite chocolate spread. I love the tart taste of yogurt against the creamy sweetness of chocolate. I don't miss corn flakes or the soft-boiled eggs and orange juice of my childhood. Then I go next door to Bet Emmanuel to join Benjamin, Reuben, and Shmuel for an hour or two of more Bible study.

They often have guests, especially on the weekends. One frequent visitor is Manny, a German Jew. He was born in Berlin, but immigrated to the United States as a teenager, so his English is American accented. He is handsome in a northern European way, and older than the brothers or me, probably in his early forties. He has already served his time in the Israeli Army, something the brothers have yet to do. Manny knows the Bible backward and forward and often takes the lead in our discussions. But I suspect something is amiss. I have to pinch myself awake as he talks on and on because his voice is mesmerizing. The brothers don't seem to notice anything, so I say nothing. But the experience I gained in Waco about spiritual discernment makes me keep my distance from him.

The summer passes uneventfully and the time comes for Arieh and Mary and baby Sarah to return. Once again I need a place to live, but Providence is working for me. Benjamin, Reuben, and Shmuel have been called up by the Army Reserves and must go for basic training. They knew it was coming, because all men in Israel must serve from age eighteen to fifty-five, either active duty or the reserves.

I move next door and house-sit for them. The move is simple because all I own are two skirts and a few blouses. They assign me a small bedroom with no closet, typical of houses in Israel. I hang my clothing on two nails on the back of the door. For companionship, I have Mary and Arieh, plus a few friends I have made in the village, one being Rachel, the brothers' cousin.

Basic training proves to be no easy task for these three Jewish boys from New York. It's not because they are not rough and fit (they're not, but soon will be). It's because they believe God's redemptive love includes the Arabs. They're not pacifist in the universal sense. If they were, they could refuse to serve. They simply took a vow in the name of Jeshua HaMashiac not to carry a weapon.

When they return from the first six weeks of basic training, their faces are burnt brown by the desert sun and wind. They are slimmer and more muscular. But the real changes are not physical. I detect a look of sadness in Benjamin's eyes. I wonder what could have caused this. It disturbs me to see this, but I figure he will tell me when he is ready.

Over dinner, the usual Sabbath chicken stew, Reuben does most of the talking. "We told our commanding officer that we would not do weapons training. We explained how God has told us not to carry arms. The officer was amazed but not angry."

"He assigned us to the medics corps," Shmuel adds.

Benjamin reluctantly picks up the narrative. "Word spread through the camp that we love Arabs." He pauses and sighs. "That night a soldier came up to me in the mess hall and spit in my face." Benjamin's voice is low, with no emotion.

Now I understand the shame and anguish in his eyes. I gasp with shock.

"What did you do then?" I ask in a small voice.

"I wiped my face and went on eating. The next day on the parade grounds, the commanding officer spoke to everyone on the base by loud speaker. '*We have three Jews among us who refuse to take up weapons. I wish I could do the same, but I can not. Any soldier who abuses them will have to answer to me*'."

During my first year living with the brothers, Mary's prayers for her husband are answered. On her daughter Sarah's birthday, after a long day that included a little party, Mary asks Arieh to say something encouraging and positive. He then calmly tells her that he now believes in Messiah Jesus.

Mary can't wait to tell her neighbors next door. I hear a knock and invite them inside. Mary whispers that Arieh has something to tell everybody in the house. The brothers are still sitting at the kitchen table when Arieh shares the good news. I honestly didn't expect to see this day, but I'm happy for Mary. Still, I can't help contrast her situation with mine. Why hasn't God answered my prayers? Why did Mansoor so vehemently reject the claims of Christ? I hug Mary and keep my private sorrow to myself. My miserable marriage and my grief over the loss of my children are not a burden I want to lay on her.

Our little community of believers is growing. We are now two households. Manny, the handsome German Jew, is there almost every weekend. Even Yassar comes occasionally for a visit. I reluctantly make a truce with him for the sake of the others. He is truly what is called in Hebrew a *misken*, or pitiful one. He tried to join an Arab Baptist Church in East Jerusalem, but the Christian Arabs distrust Muslims, even ex-Muslims. They would not receive him into their fellowship. He is still a troubled young man in search of God.

Then one day, a woman who calls herself Etty arrives on the doorstep of Bet Emmanuel. Etty is destined to change all of us in ways we never would have dreamed possible. She is tall with a full bosom. She wears her hair short, which shows off her deeply tanned face to advantage. Her energy level is high as she talks for two hours about her life and how God commissioned her to come to Israel.

"I was born in America to Jewish parents. God revealed to me that, like the Biblical Esther, I will deliver my people from evil. I'm divorced with two sons, ages ten and twelve."

Up to this point, I'm only half listening to her. Now she has my full attention—she said she has *two sons*.

"God told me to come to Israel."

Oh my Lord, she is so like me. I'm getting more and more excited.

"Then God told me to give custody of my boys to their father."

What? I can't believe I'm hearing this. My lips tighten in a straight line. Tears sting the back of my eyes. How can she voluntarily give up her children? I don't believe God has sent her to Israel. But as I look around at the faces of the brothers, even Mary and Arieh, I see that they are enthralled with her story, believing every word of it.

I'm so distraught that I excuse myself and go to my bedroom and close the door. Nervous tension reaches the breaking point, and I cry a torrent of tears. Then I hear the door softly open and Shmuel comes into the room.

"Sharona, what's wrong?"

I wipe my eyes and search my pockets for a tissue. Shmuel hands me his handkerchief. After blowing my nose, I shake my head, embarrassed about this outburst of emotion.

"Something is wrong. Etty's not telling the truth," I stammer.

Shmuel puts his arms around me and gives me a warm, brotherly hug. "I don't know what to say. She seems sincere, and the people who gave her our address are above reproach."

I'm suspicious that Manny is not who he claims to be, and now I'm doubting Etty's story. Maybe there is something wrong with me. Why am I so distrustful?

"I guess Etty's giving up her children is too painful for me to think about. I'll be all right." I go to the washroom and splash cold water on my face to hide the traces of my outburst, then return to the sitting room.

Etty stays for the weekend, sharing my little bedroom. Before she leaves on Sunday morning, she announces at breakfast that the Lord has given her a Scripture for us.

"And all that believed were together and had all things in common."

It's months before we see her again, but the words she imparted have left a deep impression. Especially with Benjamin, the unofficial leader of our group.

"I believe the Lord is leading us to share not only our daily lives, but everything. Etty's word about sharing all things in common only confirms this."

"You mean pool our money?" Shmuel looks skeptical.

"What about Arieh and Mary?" Reuben asks.

"Yes, them too." Benjamin answers.

"But we don't have any money," I protest. It's winter and the fruit packing house is closed. We might have twenty shekels between us. I don't know about this new plan of his. Especially since it is Etty's idea.

"God will provide," Benjamin says resolutely. "Beginning today."

The week passes uneventfully. No check arrives in the mail as everyone is hoping. No small jobs are offered to any of us. Our money dwindles down to nothing. Benjamin is visibly depressed. On Thursday, he announces, "If there is no chicken for our usual Sabbath meal, I'll consider this experiment in faith over."

We normally eat rice and vegetables, bread and yogurt. But Friday night we always have a chicken. It's a Jewish thing, I guess. And it will shame us not to have any food on the table for our guests.

Friday morning comes. Reuben goes to check the mail, hoping for a reprieve. But he returns empty handed. The local grocery store stays open until four. Three o'clock comes, and it looks like there will be no dinner to set before out guests. Benjamin is lying down, too depressed to talk. Reuben and Shmuel go for a walk in the fields, hoping to find something to eat, maybe money, anything.

We've been waiting for God to drop money from heaven, but I know where there is a bit of cash. Weeks earlier, I found a leather coin purse behind the bookcase in my bedroom. I figured someone had stashed it there for a special reason. So I left it alone.

Now, I have only minutes to act if I want to buy a chicken before the grocery closes. I decide this is the time to retrieve that coin purse. I move the bookcase and pull it out. I count the bill and coins. There is enough to buy food for a week.

"Benjamin, come here!" I shout.

He runs into my bedroom looking disheveled, hair sticking up this way and that.

"I've found some money," I say, pretending that I've just discovered it.

"Praise God. It's the miracle we've been waiting for." Benjamin takes the coin purse and counts out the money. We run over to the little store and buy what we need. When Reuben and Shmuel come in from the fields, the smell of sautéed onions, garlic, and stewing chicken permeates the house.

Our guests arrive, and it is a Sabbath dinner like no other. We sing songs far into the night. Arieh and Mary are informed of the miracle of the coin purse, but the other guests are told nothing. Our community of believers is now fully launched on a walk of faith. Everyone is almost giddy with joy.

Except me. I have a heavy heart. I don't consider it a miracle. I knew the money was there all along. But for the others, it is a big turning point. Especially for Reuben and Benjamin. They will continue this walk of faith for the rest of their lives, and successfully, too. I, on the other hand, will struggle with my doubts and misgivings about God's providence for years to come. It has something to do with waiting for the miracle that will allow me to hold my children once again.

Winter in the upper Galilee is mild. All I need is a heavy sweater or light jacket. We heat the living room with a kerosene heater, and the bedrooms remain without heat. It reminds me of Teheran. December seventh is Rodwin's sixteenth birthday. I wonder how he will celebrate. I can't picture him as a teenager. It seems like a dream that I have children. Soon it's December twenty-fifth. The brothers don't celebrate with a tree or presents, although we do sing Christmas hymns together. I don't mind not celebrating holidays or birthdays. That part of my life has passed.

Spring comes early to the Galilee. The almond trees blossom in late February, near Shadwin's birthday. He is ten years old this year. Just over six years difference between them. Rodwin writes once or twice a year, but Shadwin doesn't know how to write in English, and I never learned to read or write Farsi.

In summer the grass dies and turns brown. We don't even have a fan to stir the sultry air, but the thick walls of the old farmhouse keep out most of the heat.

A new family is joined to our little community of believers. They are Sabras, native Israelis, unlike the rest of us who are either American or British. Shaul and Zahava met and fell in love while both were serving in the army. They now have two sons; *Barak*, Thunder; and *Raam*, Lightning.

Shaul has had dreams of the Messiah ever since he was a young boy. When he heard that the tractor driver, Arieh, was now a follower of Messiah Yeshua, he felt compelled to come and ask questions.

"I'm not the only Jew who believes like this. Everyone in the house next door does also," Arieh tells him.

"Take me to them," Shaul commands. He is tall, barrel chested, with thick black hair and a heavy beard. He looks like a rabbi.

As if it were something he was born to, Shaul meets the brothers, then accepts the Lord as his Savior and goes home to tell his wife. Zahava has her doubts, but is willing to come for a Sabbath meal to meet us.

The night before the dinner, Zahava has a dream where she meets the Heavenly Bridegroom. After dinner she confides this to Reuben, who is astounded. He never discusses esoteric Christian theology about the Bridegroom with seekers or new believers. The scriptural concept of the Church being the Bride and Christ the Bridegroom is an easily misunderstood allegory. But the Holy Spirit has apparently prepared Zahava to accept this concept. Before the evening is over, she is professing faith in Jeshua, her Heavenly Bridegroom.

Shaul and Zahava's decision to follow Jeshua sets off a storm of protest in the village. It's one thing for the English and Americans to follow this strange religion. But Israelis? Never! The hippies in the upper village stay out of the debate, but the conservative farmers now regard us as the enemy. The local rabbi has begun to speak out against us. Children call me *missionaire* and throw rocks when I pass their playground. A sharp pebble hits my ankle and cuts the skin. I stop and glare at them. What should I do? I want to retaliate and throw a rock back, but I can't because I'm the adult here. I turn and walk swiftly out of their throwing range.

A short time later, Mary receives a strong impression from the Lord during her private prayer time. She hesitates to call it a prophecy, but that is what it is. Arieh is serving his mandatory six weeks in the reserves, so she comes and tells me. I suggest that she reveal her vision to the others next door.

"At midnight, men in black coats and hats will attack your house," she warns us.

"But how can you be so precise? Midnight?" Reuben asks.

"Are you positive?" Benjamin questions.

"Nonsense!" Manny states emphatically. "God does not speak through a woman."

"He only speaks through men?" I stand up for Mary, although I too wonder if she has gotten this message right. After all, she is a rather new believer.

Benjamin says he is going to take Mary at her word and stay alert.

After dinner we gather in the living room. At 10:00 P.M. Manny goes to bed saying, "I expect to sleep soundly." Yassar follows suit, leaving Benjamin, Reuben, Shmuel, and me sitting there.

"Mary is alone with Sarah this evening. I'm going over to keep her company," I announce.

"Good idea, Sharona. This is going to be a long night." Benjamin looks troubled.

Mary looks relieved to see me and puts on the kettle to make tea. Sarah is sleeping soundly in her cot. The clock ticks loudly on the wall. We make small talk, avoiding the issue that hangs heavy in the air. *Is she a prophetess*?

At a quarter to twelve we sit up straighter, every nerve straining, as the booming sound of male voices vibrates in the night air.

"They've come!" Mary protectively rushes to check on Sarah.

I run out the front door and into the garden. In the moonlight I see what looks like an small army of men in black coats and black hats marching on Bet Emmanuel. They're chanting in unison, but I can't make out what they are saying.

I stand mesmerized on Mary's garden steps. She's now vindicated! The door next door opens, and Shmuel and Reuben come out followed by Benjamin. Shmuel and Reuben go into the street to confront the mob. I'm confident they will talk these men out of whatever mischief they've came to do.

In seconds, Reuben is thrown to the ground with five or six men on top of him. Another three or four are trying to throw Shmuel down, but he is too tall and strong.

"My God, they're killing Reuben," I mumble to myself. Without thinking I run into the street screaming. "If you kill him, the blood of Jesus will be on your heads!"

Startled, the men in black coats look at me. I see now that they are young men, high school or college age. They are dressed in the typical garb of Yeshiva students.

I keep screaming about the blood of Jesus. I don't know if it is that name that repels them or the fact that a woman is confronting them. They back off but don't touch me or make any effort to stop me. One young man reaches down and throws a handful of dirt in my direction.

While this is going on in the street, others push Benjamin aside and storm into the house, tossing furniture about as they rampage from room to room.

They burst into the rooms where Manny and Yassar are sleeping. Both Manny and Yassar jump out of bed, run out the back door in their underwear, and disappear into the fields behind the house. Yassar is running in fear of his life from a Jewish mob. Though they don't know he is an Arab, he doesn't realize this. Manny is running because he is a chauvinistic braggart who can't face that he is wrong and Mary is right. I also think that he is coward.

The mob streams out of the house. Those in the street release Reuben and Shmuel. Then they take off running. Evidently they have vehicles waiting for them.

After we assess the damage, no broken bones, a smashed lamp and a few damaged tables, we sit down and analyze what just took place.

"I thought they were killing you." I look at Reuben with relief and wonder.

"Jews don't kill Jews," Shmuel says rubbing a sore shoulder.

"They just wanted to scare us," Benjamin adds.

Posters go up around the village warning the "missionaries" to get out of town. Our response is to act like nothing has happened. Privately, we are chagrined because the word missionary as used in Israel is pejorative. However, when Shaul's two older brothers hear about the threats against the believers, they come for a visit.

Each one carries his army issue rifle slung across his shoulder. They go from house to house, door to door. When the occupant answers, they say, "Shaul is our little brother. We don't believe like him, but we will protect him and his family. Anybody who hurts our brother gets a bullet." Then they march to the next house.

Reuben and Benjamin are distraught when they learn of these threats. But I'm pleased that Shaul's brothers care that much. My brothers would do the same.

Then new posters go up announcing that on a certain day a demonstration will be held in front of Bet Emmanuel. Pollack, a survivor of the German camps, now an artist in the hippie colony, makes a placard denouncing the demonstrators as fascists. He and Rachel sit on our front steps during the demonstration. A neighbor woman regrets that she cowered in her bed the night of the attack and did nothing to help. She also comes to sit on the front steps in solidarity with us.

The men in black gather in the street, about thirty of them. I peek out the front window at a sea of black hats. I'm not afraid, but my knees quake, literally knocking together. An alien voice whispers in my mind, "You're not a Jew. You don't belong here." Where is that voice coming from? It's the only time I have ever felt different from my friends. *Get out of my head, Satan.*

Our little community survived the harassment of the orthodox Jews, but in the coming months we are not able to stand up to the landlords and visa bureaucrats. Within a few months, Arieh and Mary have their lease canceled. The brothers' landlord also refuses to renew their lease. No one in the village will rent to Jewish Christians.

Then it's time to have my visa renewed. It is now 1978. For four years, I've been on a temporary resident visa. Technically, I am eligible to get a permanent visa by virtue of being present in the country so long.

"Your time here is up. You have to leave," the heavyset man behind the desk says as he looks at my passport.

"How long do I have?" I'm thinking: Where will I get the money for airfare back to America?

He shrugs. "When you are ready, leave."

"No fixed date?"

"No." He smiles kindly and ends the interview.

On the way home, I try to cheer myself with the thought that I have been thrown out of better places. But that's not true. Iran was not a better place. Yes, the Israeli government is telling me to go, but the visa official here is polite, even sympathetic.

I'm sad about having to leave my spiritual family. And sadder still that I will soon have an ocean between me and my sons. But events are rapidly breaking our community up in any case. The doubts I had about Manny are now coming to fruition. Not because of the incident where he ran from the house. Anyone can be forgiven a momentary weakness. No, Manny revealed his true nature one day at the bus stop. When the driver didn't open the door for him (because the bus was full), Manny violently pounded on the window and cursed the driver with blistering words. Arieh happened to overhear the outburst and was badly shaken. After Arieh reported this disturbing incident to the brothers, Benjamin made inquiry into Manny's background. He wrote to certain Jewish believers in New York and asked what they knew about him. It turned out Manny was not a Jew as he claimed. German, yes. Jewish no. He moved from Berlin to New York, then came to Israel, lied about his background, applied for citizenship, even served in the army. Now we know he is a troubled individual with psychological problems.

Benjamin confronted Manny about his past. When he continued to lie, Benjamin told him to never show his face in Rosh Pinna again. Only Shmuel couldn't believe that Manny wasn't who he claimed to be. He defended him with vehemence. But Benjamin was adamant. Manny was not welcome in our group. I'd never heard Shmuel so much as raise his voice before, but now he shouted angrily at Benjamin and stormed out of the house. I knew things would never be the same again between us all.

Eight

So our experiment in living as first century Christians comes to an unhappy close. We all go our own way. I leave for America, God providing me with airfare through a couple of retired Christians living on a nearby horse ranch. Arieh and Mary move to Upper Nazareth. Shaul and Zahava move to Tiberias. The brothers will eventually move there, also.

On my way back to the United States, I stop over in England to visit Lesley, my friend from the WIZO Baby Home in Jerusalem. She now lives with her mother, Jean, near an old mill pond, in a country village. Here I recuperate from the nervous exhaustion that I kept at bay in the Galilee. A cup of tea in bed every morning, walks down country lanes, and lots of talk and laughter restore my drooping spirits.

Then I'm off to America, stopping for a week in Huntsville, Alabama with my Godparents, Toots and Pete. When I finally arrive in California, my sister Gail informs me that there will be a family reunion at the fairgrounds in Pomona on the weekend. My brother Marlin's family is in town from Las Vegas so that their children can compete in a horse show. The rest of my complete family will be there, also.

It's nice being with my family again. I applaud as my niece and nephew, wearing cowboy gear and riding Tennessee Walkers, win awards for horsemanship. Attending the horse show eases me back into the ambiance of Southern California and the American West.

I return to Las Vegas with my mother. The good feeling of being among my own kin lasts about a month before reality sets in. My mother and I argue all the time. She can't relate to anything I tell her about my life in Israel. Momma cuts me out of her will when she learns that I have been living with three men. Never mind that this was a Christian community, celibate in philosophy and actuality. The thought of her single daughter living with three single men is too much. To further irritate me, she now defends Mansoor.

"He was always polite to me," she says stubbornly.

To add to my chagrin, she also defends my brother Pat's ex-wife.

"But, Momma, she's a pathological liar."

"She can't help herself. It's probably inherited. Her family is Mormon, you know."

How can I argue with this logic? I can't.

It is now 1978, and I realize I don't have any document that shows I am legally divorced from Mansoor. I know that from his Muslim perspective it doesn't matter, as he can have four wives and any number of concubines. Somewhat belatedly, I feel the need to have proof of my status, so I file for divorce in Las Vegas.

One day, I get a letter from Shmuel. He's in the United States on an extended visit and plans to come to Las Vegas to visit his uncle.

I rent a car and pick him up at the airport, eager to see an old friend again. His visit reminds me how much I miss Israel, and I convince myself that he has come all this way just to see me. What's an uncle? I ask myself. Shmuel is tall and lanky with fuzzy red hair and freckles. His physical appearance is not what attracts women (he always had a female admirer or two in Israel). Rather, it's the way he listens, really listens when a woman talks.

One day we drive out to Lake Mead for a picnic. Another evening, we take in a show at the newly opened MGM Grand. Now I'm acting out of character by putting my hair up in rollers at night. I still don't bother with makeup, but there is definitely a change in me. My mother begins to hope that I might get married again. I'm thinking along the same lines.

On Shmuel's last night in Las Vegas he invites me to dinner to meet his family.

"My Aunt and Uncle want to take me somewhere special. I know they will like you."

He doesn't have a car, so I drive over to the uncle's house at 7:00 P.M. I've changed clothes twice and fussed with my hairdo all afternoon. I put on my best dress and sandals (I never adjust to high heels and stockings). This will be a special evening, I can feel it.

I ring the doorbell, and his aunt answers the door. She looks surprised to see me.

"Come in. I'll get Shmuel."

After a lengthy delay, Shmuel returns with his aunt. "There's been a misunderstanding," his aunt says, adding, "This is our last night together and we want to be alone as a family."

My cheeks feel hot. I look to Shmuel for an explanation. He remains silent.

"After all, you aren't engaged, or anything," she continues awkwardly.

"No, of course not," I admit, barely able to breathe. I say good-bye and rush out the door. On the way back to my mother's home, I confront my own vulnerabilities. I wanted to believe this friendship was leading to marriage, so I imagined his interest was more than brotherly. He had never said anything about relinquishing his vow of celibacy.

When I return home by eight, my mother knows something is wrong. For once she has the tact to say nothing.

The next morning, I drive Shmuel to the airport as prearranged. He apologizes for the embarrassment he caused me the night before.

"It's nothing," I shrug. "They wanted to have you to themselves on your last night." I hope I'm hiding the humiliation I feel at my own stupidity. Shmuel may have led me on in some oblique way, but I'm not going to admit it now.

Shmuel says good-bye and hands me a gift, a straw handbag from Jamaica. I later toss it into my suitcase without opening it. (Six months later, I decide to throw it out and happen to look inside. It contains five hundred dollars in crisp one hundred notes. Shmuel's apology for the dinner fiasco?)

My mother and I still argue about everything. When I can't take it anymore, I ask my brother Marlin if I can live with him and his family until I find a job.

"Hey, you lasted longer with Meese (his pet name for our mother) than I expected. We laid bets on it." Marlin and his wife Wanda put me in their guest bedroom. It's fun being around their three teenagers who ride horses or drive cars, but do not, ever, walk. Apparently, teenagers in Las Vegas find walking demeaning. I, on the other hand, haven't owned a car for years and consider walking natural.

For the second time in my life, I decide Las Vegas is not the city for me, and I decide to go back to Waco. I stay with my friend Jewel. The people at Grace Gospel are happy to see me. Betsy even gives me a beautiful London Fog raincoat. "You'll need this wherever you live," she explains.

Then I get a letter from Etty inviting me to come back to Israel and share her apartment in Jerusalem. Even though my first impression of her had not been good, I had learned from Shmuel during his visit that she is settled in Jerusalem and keeps in close contact with Benjamin and Reuben. Putting my doubts about her behind me, I use the money Shmuel gave me and buy a one-way ticket to Tel Aviv. But first I must go back to Las Vegas and make amends with my mother. She's forgotten we even quarreled, she tells me.

While in Las Vegas, I receive a mysterious telephone call from a woman in San Diego. She says she's a friend of the family and knows where my son Rodwin is.

"He's in Teheran. Why are you calling me?" My fingers grip the phone until the tips turn white.

"Your son is not in Iran."

"Where is he then?" Anxiety turns to hope.

"California."

My knees grow weak, causing me to sit on a chair while I continue talking.

"Where in California?"

"I promised Mansoor I wouldn't tell you. But I feel sorry for you. I'm also a mother."

"Then tell me where he is!"

"I'll have Rodwin call you tonight."

I'm holding the receiver in my hand with the dial tone buzzing. My mother looks at me and asks what's wrong.

"Rodwin is in California. He'll call me tonight."

Conflicting emotions surge through my heart. Is he really here? How? Why? Maybe this woman is playing a cruel joke. I can hardly breathe.

"Momma, I'm going out for a walk." I burn off my nervous energy by walking for two hours. First I believe it's true and I'm overjoyed. Then I think it's a joke and want to cry. I stay by the phone all evening. At 9:00 P.M., I pick up the receiver on the first ring.

"Hello?"

"This is Rodwin." He pronounces it Rod-ween. I don't recognize his voice. But of course he is a teenager now and his voice has changed.

"How do I know this is really you?" I begin to cry softly.

"Shareen, it's me." He's always called me that, even as a toddler.

"Where are you?" I am crying harder now.

"I can't tell you. I promised I wouldn't contact you when I got to America."

"You're in California." It's a statement not a question.

"Ah . . . yes."

I can tell by his voice that he's beginning to get nervous. I know his father has poisoned him against me.

"I have to hang up now," Rodwin says abruptly.

"Call me tomorrow!" I shout into the phone.

I collapse on the couch and repeat to my mother each word Rodwin said. I'm deeply relieved he is safe in the United States. It is 1979. The revolution against the Shah of Iran is in full swing, and Americans are being held hostage in the American Embassy. The same Embassy where Rodwin got his cholera shots so many years ago. Only last week, I saw pictures of the British Embassy going up in flames. Mansoor's home is only a few miles from there, so I called and asked to talk to Rodwin. He said Rod was asleep. Other times when I called, he said Rod was at school or out playing. Now, I know why I could never reach him. He's in America!

Rodwin calls again the next night. I ask him about Shadwin. He assures me that his little brother is safe.

"Why can't you tell me where you're staying?"

"My father says you might kidnap me."

"Oh, for the love of God!" I exclaim.

"Sorry, Shareen, but I promised."

He sounds adamant and I don't know how to convince him that I pose no threat. I think of my travel plans and how I'm returning to Jerusalem in one week. Deep sadness overwhelms me. We are so close, yet so far apart. I don't want to cry but I can't hold the tears back.

"I guess that's it then. I'm leaving for Jerusalem next week. I'll never see you again."

There is a long pause. Then Rodwin answers, "I suppose it will be all right for you to visit me before you go."

I had said the magic words. I'm leaving the country and therefore would not pose a threat.

"Give me your address."

"Ah," he stammers and struggles a minute. "I have a soccer game this Saturday. You can meet me there."

I've waited nine years for this. I'll meet him on the soccer field, I'll meet him on the moon if that is where he thinks he is safe. He then gives me the directions to a soccer field in San Diego.

I book a plane ticket to Los Angeles. My sister, Gail, and her husband, John, pick me up at LAX and take me to their house in Arcadia, not far from our childhood home. They are delighted that I will soon be reunited with at least one of my boys. My younger sister Kim agrees to drive me to San Diego early Saturday morning. She knows how much this means to me and brings her camera to record the reunion of mother and son.

I stand behind the wire fence watching a group of young men playing soccer. They all look Middle Eastern. I recognize him right away. Rodwin stands out because he is taller than his peers. Always was, I note proudly. With his mustache, he reminds me of a young Clark Gable.

He comes over to the fence and I throw my arms around him and hug him tightly. He doesn't resist. In fact he hugs me back.

"Let's go somewhere we can talk," he says.

"You mean your mother is more important than the game?" I'm serious, not joking. By now I take nothing for granted.

We get in Kim's car and he suggests a Spanish restaurant that has a beautiful courtyard with fountains and palm trees. I can't take my eyes off him. He is so handsome. So slender. He hasn't filled out yet with his full growth. Kim takes picture after picture as we stroll in the garden, stopping by a fountain, or admiring the flowers.

It's as if the long, sad years have slipped away. They are gone as if they never occurred. The bond between mother and child is there, strong as ever. I see my love for him beaming back to me in his eyes. Nothing Mansoor has said or done can alter that.

Over our lunch on the patio, Rodwin tells us how he narrowly escaped being drafted and sent to fight the Iraqis.

"On my next birthday, I'll turn eighteen. Dad didn't want me to be drafted so he arranged for me to study in the United States."

I know from the news reports that the carnage on the Iraqi-Iranian front is high. Most of the casualties are teenage boys, like Rodwin. On this point, I concur with Mansoor.

"The same day I flew out of Teheran, Khomeini flew in and took over the country. The first thing he did was shut the airport."

"So you got out just in time." I say, only now comprehending what danger Rodwin had been in.

"My Swissair flight left so quickly, there was no time for the caterer's truck to supply food. All we ate were chocolate bars until we got to Geneva."

"Thank God, you're here. But what about Shadi?"

"He'll be safe until he turns fourteen. They take boys even that young. But maybe things will be better, now that the Shah is gone."

"Anyone is better than the Shah," I say, not knowing what I'm talking about.

"Let's have an Ayatollah-cola and drink to the next dictator," Kim says.

Rodwin laughs at her joke. I'm pleased to see he has retained his love of word play. When he was younger he always enjoyed making word games by mixing Farsi and English. The *ayatollah-cola* pleases him.

I'm full of questions for him.

"Did you support the revolution?

"No, but I don't like the Shah, if that's what you mean."

"How were you treated during all the anti-American demonstrations?"

A crooked smile appears. "Over there I'm a damned American. Here I'm a damned *Eye-ranian.*"

"What grade is Shadi now? Does he remember any English?"

"A little, but he speaks only Farsi."

Does he remember me?" I hold my breath hardly unable to bear what I may hear next.

"He knows you as the lady who sends toys and clothes occasionally."

I blink back the tears, determined that nothing will mar this perfect day.

I'm about to travel to the other side of the world, at the very moment when I have finally been reunited with my son. My mother doesn't understand it. She thinks I should cancel my plans to return to Jerusalem.

"I can't." I tell her. "Rodwin only agreed to reveal his whereabouts because I am leaving. His peace of mind is based on the fact that I will not be around to interfere in his life."

I have a few clues regarding the garbage his father has stuffed into his head all these years. A relative in Iran once wrote and asked if it was true that I hit Shadwin in the eye. I know the kind of slander Mansoor is capable of.

I have plans to live in Jerusalem, and I'm not going to change them now, causing Rodwin to suspect me of lying. Plus, I can see that he turned out (despite his father) to be a splendid young man, with his feet firmly on the ground. He is on his own for the first time in his life and enjoying himself immensely.

When he first arrived in San Diego, he lived with the woman who had called me in Las Vegas. Then he enrolled in a community college and met other Iranian students. Now, he shares an apartment with three other students like himself, loving his independence. He doesn't need a mother hovering over his shoulder, as much as I would love to do so. I accept that he is grown up. It's enough that our love for each other endured the separation.

Nine

Now, I can return to Jerusalem truly at peace. I have confidence that Mansoor will send Shadwin out of Iran when it's necessary.

After the plane reaches cruising altitude, I take out the packet of photographs of Rodwin taken in the Mexican restaurant. I gaze fondly at the pictures of my son, marveling at his height of six-feet-four. That kind of height doesn't come from his Persian genes. But then there is no one that tall in my family, either. He will be eighteen on his next birthday.

How can the years slip away so quickly? I feel like the same person, but the passage of nine years is obvious with the changes in Rodwin. I think he's a handsome young man, but that might be a mother's bias. He looks more like my side of the family. His hair is dark brown, not black, nor does he have the trademark heavy Persian eyebrows. Before I left, he promised to answer all my letters. Now that he is free of his father's domination, I believe he will.

When my plane approaches Tel Aviv, I mentally switch gears. I've learned over the years to compartmentalize and can do it with ease. My children are my precious, but hidden, treasures, like a perfect melody I keep in my heart and can never sing. Mansoor belongs to an episode I am determined never to think of. Life in Israel is an exciting time of new possibilities where the recent past does not exist. And not only for me. Maybe this is partially why I fit in so well in Israel.

Etty will be at the airport to meet me. In the year that I have been gone, her life has taken some unexpected paths. It all began in the residential Ulpan where she studied Hebrew with other new immigrants like her. But not *exactly* like her. Etty is a Jew who believes in Jesus Christ. If she had kept quiet about her beliefs, she would have finished her course, received her citizenship papers, and gone on with her life.

The one person she confided in told the head of the school that they have a "Jew for Jesus" in their midst. Etty was expelled from the Ulpan, and the government refused to grant her citizenship.

As she wrote to me, "I have as much right as any Jew to stay here." Perhaps it's her American background, or her own brand of chutzpah, but Etty hired a lawyer and took her case as far as the Supreme Court of Israel.

The court ruled against her when it was revealed that she had been baptized by a minister in the United States and had officially changed her religion. Nevertheless, they gave her a permanent resident permit, allowing her to stay in the country.

I would not have considered rooming with Etty (I still remember the doubts I had about her when I lived in the Galilee), if it were not for the fact that Reuben and Benjamin supported her legal battles. In fact, they are now her spiritual mentors.

The plane taxis to a stop on the tarmac. As I descend the portable staircase, I lift my face to smell the orange blossoms from a nearby grove. It's good to be back. I pause and revel in the moment even though I'm worried about facing the passport control officer. What does he have on the computer? Do I have a black mark against my name because of my activities in the Galilee? I've heard of Christians who were not allowed to enter Israel. Christian tourists are welcome with opened arms. However so called *missionaries*, who, by popular belief, bribe Jews to convert are not welcome.

I fill out the official form. First name, last name, and father's first name: Sharon, daughter of Nathan. This looks kosher enough to me. My Jewish-sounding names are probably why they previously granted me temporary residence. I believe that God has allowed me to come back to Jerusalem, and He will see that I get the necessary visa. I do. The clerk stamps my passport with the famous Israeli indifference, and I move through the line without his even looking at me.

Etty is waiting at the rail, furiously waving to me. Her large brown eyes light up, and I know she is genuinely pleased to see me. I wave back, and I'm struck with the similarities. We're both around the same age, height, and weight. She has two sons and so do I. The only visible difference between us is my long hair contrasted with her short cap of curls.

On the drive up to Jerusalem, I recognize familiar landmarks. First, the Monastery at Latrun where the monks tend the vineyards. As the hills get steeper and the road winds back and forth, the pine trees of the Jerusalem Forest grow closer to the highway. I inhale their sweet, piney fragrance. Old rusted tanks from the War of Independence are still there as a reminder that Jerusalem was besieged in 1967. In the distance, I can see the white stone buildings, almost ethereal in the thin sunlight.

"My home is in a new neighborhood called Ramot," Etty tells me. "It's one of the many new apartment developments circling Jerusalem. They're built for strategic purposes."

"In the event of renewed hostilities with the Palestinians?"

"Right."

As we approach Ramot, I see what she means. The streets are arranged in concentric circles. The three-story buildings are made of the famous Jerusalem stone. Windows are small and narrow, easily defensible. It's a modern day fortress masquerading as a quiet neighborhood. Because it's new, the trees are small, but the numerous gardens and playgrounds are filled with flowers and green grass.

Her second floor apartment is light and airy. The furnishings are simple: a wicker sofa and love seat with flower-splashed coverings. Etty shows me to the spare bedroom. There is a single cot, an armoire, and a small desk.

After a restless night due to the time changes, I wake at dawn. I hear birds chirping through the open window. The sun is shining. The sky is cloudless. It all seems so perfect, and I'm glad to be back in Jerusalem, even in the suburbs. I sit up in bed and read the Psalms of David. Then I make my daily petition for God to watch over and keep Rodwin and Shadwin.

At seven o'clock, I throw on a bathrobe and go to the kitchen for coffee.

"Good morning." Etty greets me, already smartly dressed in a skirt and blouse and shoes to match.

"You're up and ready to go?" I laugh, looking down at my bedroom slippers and robe.

"I may be interviewed by the local press this morning. I want to be ready."

"Is this about your court case?"

"Yes."

"This is all very exciting. Reporters coming to the apartment and all," I say as I make the coffee.

"The Lord wants you to be fully dressed by 7:00 A.M., as I am," Etty says curtly, smoothing her skirt.

"Sure, Etty. I can do that." She doesn't have to use God as an excuse. If she doesn't want me sitting around in a bathrobe, fine. I feel a prickle of annoyance but shrug it off.

I return to my bedroom to dress. First, I put on my favorite long skirt and tee shirt. After looking in the mirror, I decide a calf length skirt is more appropriate. I don't want to appear like a hippie. I have a lot to do my first day back. But first I'm meeting old friends in the city.

The always crowded Atara Cafe near King David Street is the most popular coffee house in Jerusalem. The waiters are old men from another era, who wear black gabardine trousers and stiffly starched shirts. The aroma of freshly baked rolls and rich coffee gives me a sense of well being.

I greet my friends who are already seated near the window. Esther, originally from Rhodesia, is one of the first friends I made in Israel. She's sitting beside her husband Dard, now the pastor at the Garden Tomb. She is petite, with light brown hair and green eyes. They make a handsome couple, sitting at the little table with the sunlight on their heads like a benediction.

"Welcome back, Sharon. How are things going with you and Etty in Ramot?"

"Great," I reply. I decide not to mention the irritation I felt earlier with Etty.

I look at the menu and order *cafe afook*, upside-down coffee. I love this version of hot, frothy milk mixed with expresso. The others order the same.

Animated conversation buzzes around the cafe like a friendly swarm of bees. Everybody is talking at once, and I can hear at least three or four different languages being spoken.

"Speaking of Etty, we have something to tell you." Dard glances at his wife while the waiter places our coffee cups on the table with the precision of a watchmaker.

"Yes?" I quit fussing with a packet of brown sugar, alert because of the subtle change in his voice.

"Sharon, you know Dard is a member of the local Pastors Association." Esther squeezes his hand. They're so in love. It makes me feel good to see it.

"We meet once a month to discuss concerns within the local churches here in Jerusalem," Dard continues.

"And?" I don't know how this concerns me, but I'm worried because they look so grave.

"Your new housemate has caused considerable controversy among us."

"Because she took her case to the Supreme Court?"

"No, although when she came to us for counsel, we told her not to push the issue of citizenship." Dard pauses to tell the elderly waiter to bring us lemon cheesecake. Only when he walks away does Dard continue. "It's a far more serious matter than citizenship."

"I already know about the rumors."

"You do?" They look at each other with relief written on their faces.

"Etty told me about the slander. Rumors of sexual impropriety. I don't believe a word of it. She *is* odd. But she's as strait-laced as a deacon's wife."

Dard and Esther again look at each other, shaking their heads.

"We're concerned for *your* reputation, Sharon. We think you should get your own place."

"But why?" I'm truly puzzled. "The brothers have made no mention of any trouble with Etty other than her legal difficulties."

"I'm going to tell it to you straight. Etty suffers from delusions. Spiritual manifestations of aggrandizement."

"What?" There is abhorrence in his voice that I can't understand.

"She believes she is the sole, physical Bride of Christ."

"Nonsense!" I laugh out loud with nervous relief. "It's going to be only Etty dressed in white at the Marriage Supper of the Lamb? It's just more gossip."

"All right, Sharon, do what you think best. We won't mention this again." My friend pats my hand reassuring me that our relationship will continue whether I take their advice or not.

To break the tension, we dig into our cheesecake and eat every last crumb. Then I mention that I'm actively job hunting.

"I was a bookkeeper for the United Nations in Teheran, but as you know, I can't get a work permit for any job that an Israeli could do." I wipe my chin with a thin sheet of paper that is masquerading as a napkin.

"Try Saint Louis Hospice."

"What is it?"

"A Catholic hospice for the terminally ill. They always need workers." Dard adds.

"Yeah, well I guess Israelis aren't eager to work there, it being Catholic and all." I'm not so sure I want to work there, either. But it's a lead and I can't afford to be picky.

The following day I look up at the granite statue of Saint Louis. I've passed this building many times and never knew it was a hospital. More precisely, it's a hospice, which I've learned is a hospital, or sometimes a hotel, run by a religious organization. The three-story stone building, opposite New Gate and left of Barclays Bank, is on the border between East Jerusalem and West Jerusalem. The walls are pockmarked with bullet holes from the Six Day War.

I enter the main door and find myself in a large hall with high ceilings and carved cornices. This might have been a posh hotel during the British Mandate. There is no front desk and I don't see a soul. Taking the wide, marble staircase, I go upstairs. Hesitantly, I walk down the long corridor, glancing into rooms on either side. Sick people are sleeping or sitting in metal beds painted the color of shiny green apples. The walls are painted the same color. The white tiled floor is spotless. The air is suffused with the usual sickroom smells of vomit, excrement, and disinfectant. I detect something else, the sweetish smell of decay.

A nursing sister comes out of one of the rooms with her arms full of soiled laundry and says something to me in French.

"I don't speak French."

"Can I help you?"she replies in passable English. Her nun's habit is blue with a matching veil that comes to her shoulders. Her eyes are gray and they sparkle with good humor, despite the smelly bundle she is holding.

"Do you need a nurse's aide?"

She nods vigorously. "*Oui*, speak to our superior," she says and motions with her shoulder down the corridor.

I find the head nurse, or Mother Superior. I'm not sure how to address her. She quickly puts me at ease by saying that she desperately needs help.

"When can you start?"

"Now?"

"Good. We pay a small salary and provide all your meals." She calls a subordinate to show me around.

I don't know if I'm relieved or worried about finding a job so quickly.

Before I have time to consider what I'm doing, I'm wearing a stiffly starched white apron and pushing a tea cart from room to room. Each room holds four beds. Those who can sit up welcome the hot cup of tea and cookies I'm passing around.

By dinner time, I have the sense of the people in Saint Louis'. Eighty percent of the patients are Jews, twenty percent Arabs. I learn this by trial and error, speaking first in Hebrew. If they don't respond, I speak the few words of Arabic I know. The nursing staff are nuns from a French order. The kitchen and cleaning staff are Arabs. There are other workers like myself, mostly young Germans who have volunteered to work in Israel for a season.

I notice one patient in particular, an elderly Arab man with a young wife sitting by his bedside. He has not touched his dinner tray. I put it on the cart and return it to the kitchen with the other dirty dishes.

At my dinner break, I'm dismayed to find the kitchen has sent me the very meal the elderly man had refused to eat. "I can't eat this," I tell a German volunteer sitting in the staff dining room.

She smiles broadly, as if this was a test of some kind. "No problem. I never eat the food the patients get either. The cook thought you, being American, would eat anything."

"What do you have?" I eye her plate of flat bread and bowl of sauce.

"Babaganoush. Have some."

I like eggplant, so I sit down and join her. When we're through, she shows me how to return the dishes to the kitchen on the dumb waiter. The patient's uneaten meal is sent back the same way. I learn later that the old man who couldn't eat his dinner died that night.

I quickly pick up the routine of daily care: helping the patients take a shower, serving meals, changing sheets, and giving back rubs. But it's not like working at the Baby Home where each child had a rosy future. These people have come here to die. They've gone the route of aggressive medical care, and now there is no surgery or medical intervention left.

In the Catholic tradition of service to God, these nursing nuns devote their lives to Saint Louis' patients. They sleep on the third floor, work on the second floor, and their chapel is on the ground floor. They're never out of range of the sounds of suffering, day or night. I'm not like them. When my shift is over, I eagerly go back to Etty's cheerful apartment in Ramot.

"Etty, some friends are in town. I've invited them to lunch today," I say while washing up the breakfast dishes. "You'll like Toots and Pete. They're my spiritual parents."

"You've mentioned them before. He's retired Air Force, right?"

"Yes, and she's a Jewish believer, like yourself." I hang the damp dish towel on the clothesline outside the kitchen window.

"I also have spiritual mentors," adds Etty. "They live in Boston, but will be coming to Jerusalem soon."

Toots and Pete look exactly like they did when I saw them last in Huntsville; white-haired, thin, wiry, and full of energy. I introduce them to my roommate. Toots greets Etty with a warm hug. Pete shakes her hand. His military bearing and posture are consistent with his West Point background. I smile at him, and there is a twinkle in his eyes as he smiles back. I love this man. An officer and a gentleman of the first order.

After they're seated in the living room, I go to make the sandwiches. I can hear their conversation through the open kitchen door.

"Tell me all about yourself, darling," Toots begins. "Sharon tells me you have quite a story."

Etty recounts every detail of her recent court case. When she brings her narrative to the present, she stands up. "This is too important to tell sitting down."

That's strange, I tell myself. What's too important? I stop what I'm doing and go to observe from the doorway. Etty is standing in the middle of the living room, facing my friends.

"God had chosen me for a special task." She straightens her shoulders, thrusting her chest forward like a ship in full sail.

Oh no, I groan. Not the Bride of Christ thing again.

"I will lead the Russian Jews out of slavery," Etty says majestically.

"And bring them back to Israel?" Toots' voice reveals skepticism.

"Yes, I'm a modern day Moses, you might say." Etty is still standing in the center of the room.

I exhale in relief that she didn't bring up the *bride* thing. But the respite is fleeting, for the truth hits me like a fist in the stomach.

She *is* delusional. Turning back to the kitchen, I sit at the Formica table with my head in my hands. My dreams of a life shared with Etty fly out the window, disappearing in the harsh light of day. Once again, I've teamed up with a crazy person. Do I stay on as her roommate, or leave?

At the kitchen table, with the makings of tuna salad in front of me, I make up my mind to stand by her and do what I can to minimize her grandiose ideas. I will be the voice of reason in her life. When she talks as though she is a modern day Moses or Queen Esther, I will gently restore her to the real world.

That summer, Etty's friends come from Boston to visit her. Sid is a pastor of a small inner-city church. He is accompanied by his wife and a small group from their church. I look forward to their visit so that I can talk to Pastor Sid, heart to heart, about Etty's mental state.

For months now, Etty has been speaking in church groups and prayer meetings about her mission to Russia. As word of her mission spreads, the mailbox is full of letters and checks, not only from Israel but from all over the world. She exerts incredible charisma when she stands in front of an audience. Evangelical Christians must be the most gullible people on earth. I know she is conning her audiences, but I don't know what to do about it.

Before I have a chance to speak with Pastor Sid, a woman in the group from his church asks to meet with me privately. I have some misgivings, but I arrange to meet her at a tea shop in the Old City after my shift at Saint Louis.

The woman I meet in the tea shop is dressed in tailored slacks and a bright silk blouse. She and her fellow parishioners are on a tour of the Holy Land with Pastor Sid. I wonder what she has to say to me. It must be about Etty. Lately, everything is about her.

"I've been Etty's friend and confidante for over two years." She speaks softly, hardly above a whisper. Clearly something is bothering her. She raises her head and looks in my eyes as if to judge whether it's safe to continue.

"I'm Etty's friend, also. We're on the same side," I say, encouraging her to open up.

"When Etty lived in Boston, she told me certain things." The woman warms her hands on the hot glass of tea as if she's cold. She is around my age, with short blond hair and the tan of a regular tennis player. "Did you know that Etty is God's chosen one?"

I pause, not sure I want to hear what is coming next. Surely, she isn't bringing up that old story about being the Bride of Christ?

"I know Etty has a problem in some areas. For instance, she fantasizes about being a Moses type. I want to speak to Pastor Sid about it." I speak in the most noncommittal voice I can manage.

"No, it's not that. I mean . . . " She gulps her tea and winces, clearly burning her tongue.

"Just say what you mean." When I see her reaction, I pat her hand to apologize for my abruptness. This mollifies her enough to continue.

"Etty *is* the Bride of Christ." She sets her glass down on the table with a loud crack. People at nearby tables look up with surprise. "There. I've said it, though I promised her I wouldn't."

"The Bride again," I say dully, as I feel my gorge rise. "She isn't just a member of the Church that comprises the Bride of Christ. She's the one and only?"

"Yes."

"Don't you read your Bible?" My voice raises in annoyance. The proprietor of the tea shop looks up, alarmed.

"I've had doubts. That's why I'm telling you," she answers honestly.

"If Etty is the Bride, what does that make you?" I lower my voice trying to not attract any more attention. "Or me? At the Marriage Supper of the Lamb, will we be onlookers? Bridesmaids?"

"As her best friend, Etty said I would be like a lady-in-waiting."

"Oh, Lord, give me strength," I mutter.

"What did you say?"

"Does Pastor Sid know about this?" I ask with incredulity in my voice.

"Yes, of course."

I can't put it off any longer. That night I ask Pastor Sid and his wife to come to the apartment so that I can confront Etty in front of them.

We sit around the glass-topped table in the dining room drinking coffee. I study Pastor Sid. He is in his sixties, wearing a plain sport shirt and slacks, as is fitting a pastor of an inner-city church. Not much salary, I imagine. His church is nondenominational, which means no oversight by higher authorities. Which, in this situation, is not good. From everything Etty has told me, Sid is evangelical in doctrine and preaching. He surely knows the Scriptures better than I do.

I can't believe he has swallowed Etty's distortions. I know she can sound highly credible. She is articulate and spontaneous. I grudgingly admit her personality is warm and even charismatic. Taking a deep breath, I say what I have to say.

"Are you aware that Etty thinks she is the sole, physical Bride of Christ?"

Etty looks at me with raised eyebrows. I can see she wasn't expecting this. I ignore her. It's not her reaction that I'm keen to see, but Sid's.

He looks at his hands, smoothing a rough cuticle. He brushes a crumb off his lap before replying. "Let's go to the Word of God," he says at last.

Everyone at the table scrambles to find their Bible. I go to the bedroom and get mine. Etty does the same. When we return to the table, Sid has his Bible already opened.

"Let's turn to the Gospel of John, chapter 21, verse 22." He waits for us to find our place.

"Good," I reply. "Let's read Scripture that will bring clarity." I deliberately look at Etty, then silently read the passage. Sid's wife and Etty do the same.

"Let me recap," Sid says after we finish reading the passage. "After the resurrection, Jesus reveals to Peter the manner of death he will suffer on His behalf. Then Peter asks what will happen to John. Jesus says, in effect, 'If I have chosen him for a special task, what is that to you?'" Sid looks pointedly at me.

"I'm not following you, Sid. What has this to do with Etty being the Bride of Christ?"

"Don't you see? If God has chosen Etty, *what is that to you*?"

I'm dumbstruck. I can't answer such an audacious misinterpretation of Scripture. And by a pastor who should know better. I sit there in amazed silence. Then I excuse myself saying, "I have to go to the bathroom."

I splash cold water on my face in an effort to stanch the nausea. Then I go to my bedroom. I lie face down, crying into the pillow so they won't hear me. I'd thought I was strong enough to help Etty. I'm not. In the months that I've been in her home, I've never even come close to convincing her that she's mistaken. Now, I feel that I'm in danger. It has happened to good people like Pastor Sid and his wife. The brothers are not evil or stupid. But they are blinded by her, also. If I stay one more night under her roof, I too might succumb to the twisted demons of logic that prevail in her.

I resolve to leave Etty's apartment this very night. When I go back, I find that the living room is empty. Pastor Sid must have left while I was in my bedroom. I can see the light under Etty's door. I return to my bedroom and pull a suitcase from under the bed. I travel light since I left Teheran, so it only takes fifteen minutes to pack. I scribble a note, leaving it on the kitchen counter, then slip out the front door. If I hurry, I can catch the last bus to the city.

I pay for a room at Christ Church Inn at Jaffa Gate, where I'm only a short walk from my job at Saint Louis. After falling into a fitful sleep on the narrow, metal cot, I dream that I'm lost, standing by a wild, rushing river. I don't know how to cross it but feel that I must. My distress is so great that I can't remember my own name. I awake with a start, sweat beading on my forehead, asking "Who am I?"

I go to work every day, grateful that the needs of the patients overshadow my own personal crisis. During a shift I don't have to think about myself. I don't think about Etty. I come back to my rented room at Christ Church Inn, exhausted and ready to sleep. It's a period of confusion as I reconsider why I came back to Jerusalem in the first place. It all seems an exercise in futility. In a very small way, I'm helping the sick and dying at Saint Louis, but the German volunteers work much harder than I do. My individual contribution is negligible. So, what is God's will for me? I don't know. Heaven is silent. Then I receive an aerogram from Rodwin. *Father and Shadi are on their way to California.*

I drop everything and make plans to return to California as soon as possible. Etty and her delusions are no longer my concern.

Ten

"Hi, Rod, I'm back in California." I'm speaking from a pay phone at LAX.

"Good," he laughs pleasantly. "I thought you might come back. Want to speak with Shadi?"

"Of course." I'm hyperventilating with excitement. Breathe in, slowly breathe out, I tell myself.

"Halloo?" At age thirteen, his voice is still childlike. It hasn't changed like that of his brother, who is now nineteen.

"Hello, Shadi, how was your trip?" I don't know what else to say in my anxiety and joy. What do you say to your son after ten years? So I rely on safe clichés.

There is a pause, and I hear him say to Rodwin, "What means trip?"

Oh my God! He doesn't understand English! I never thought of this during all our years apart. I hear him and Rod talking rapidly in Farsi.

"Gud," Shadi replies in answer to my question. Then Rodwin comes back on the phone.

"When can I come to your apartment? Is Mansoor there?" I have a million questions but will keep them for later.

The following day, I knock on their apartment door with fear and trembling. It's been a decade since I've seen Mansoor. I don't look forward to this meeting, but if it is the only way I can see my sons, then so be it. I'm relieved when Rodwin opens the door.

We hug, then he ushers me into the living room. Mansoor is standing in the kitchen. I start at the sight of him. His face is gaunt, with deep lines running perpendicular on his cheeks. He obviously dyes his hair black, as it was turning gray even when I first met him at the university. I'm acutely uncomfortable meeting my nemesis after all these years. Does he know how much grief he has caused me? Of course not. It's not in his nature to be reflective. I'm here to see Shadwin, I remind myself. I'll face the devil if only I can see my son again.

"Halloo, Shareen." Mansoor's voice is gravelly and hoarse, hardly above a whisper.

"Hello, Mansoor." I return his greeting, chilled by his mirthless smile. I look around and don't see Shadwin in the living room or kitchen. "Where is Shadwin?" I'm beginning to panic. Maybe it's a joke. Maybe he's still in Iran.

"He's a little bashful, so he's hiding upstairs," Rodwin reassures me. "Please, sit." He gestures towards the couch.

I pretend to watch the football game on television. Rodwin goes to the kitchen to get me a soft drink. Now and then I glance at the staircase. Then I see Shadwin sitting at the top of the stairs. When he thinks I'm not looking, he peers down at me through the banister. I blink rapidly to halt the tears that sting my eyeballs. I sneak a look at him. He does likewise to me. An invisible line connects us, like a gentle game of tug-of-war.

Rodwin serves me a glass of something cold. He begins to tell me the details of his father's and brother's escape from Iran.

"Khomeini's government is conscripting boys as young as thirteen to send to the front. The war of attrition between Iraq and Iran is continuing, you know."

"Yes, I vaguely know the details. I didn't realize it would affect Shadwin." I take a sip of my drink, which feels good on my dry throat.

"My father hatched a plan to get Shadi out of the country before he was drafted. First, he convinced the authorities that Shadwin needed surgery on his left eye to correct a serious defect in his vision. Then he proved that it can only be done by a specialist in Spain."

I grow very still, fixing my gaze on the hanging plant behind Rodwin's head. So this is the eye problem that an aunt had written to me about. She wrote that Mansoor was blaming me, telling the family that I hit Shadwin in the face when he was a baby. Anger surges in my heart, making my cheeks feel hot. With effort I will myself to be calm.

Rodwin continues, unaware of my inner turmoil. "While in Spain, Mansoor went to the American Embassy to apply for a visa to the United States. However, with Americans held hostage at the American Embassy in Teheran, visas were being denied to Iranians."

"How did you feel about that?" I ask, wondering if he identifies with the Americans or the Iranians.

"They're being well fed. No one is beating them. I don't understand why it's such a big deal."

I'm taken aback by his nonchalance, but not wanting to delve into that issue now, I ask, "So how did Mansoor get around the matter of the denied visa?"

"Shadwin has an American birth certificate." Rodwin replies.

"Yes, I went to great lengths to get it for him, against your father's objections." I drink half my cola in one big gulp. Rodwin twirls his glass. I realize he is uncomfortable when I criticize his father.

"Then my Dad convinced the Embassy clerk that Shadwin couldn't travel to America alone. He would need his father to accompany him. However, he couldn't get a visa for Salmeh."

I remember Salmeh. Mansoor hired her to take care of the house after I left. So she has been with him all these years. "Where is she?" I look around the room.

"Dad sent her back to Iran."

Well good for her, I'm thinking. She'll live in the family home and do what she pleases for a change. Now she can bring back the child Mansoor made her give up when she went to work for him.

Out of the corner of my eye, I see that Shadwin has climbed down the steps, one by one, and is now sitting on the first step. He is like a shy deer that might startle at the least movement. I continue talking with Rodwin. After a few minutes, Shadwin moves over in front of the television and stretches out to watch the game, as if I were not there.

I feast my eyes on him. He's wearing a football jersey and denim shorts like any American kid. His hair is dark like his brother's, but his features are more finely chiseled. He's so beautiful, I want to reach out and touch him. But I don't. I know I have to let him come to me. Every few minutes, he sneaks a glance at me. I'm content to let the afternoon pass in this way. I want these good feelings to continue forever.

But finally, it's time to go. Shadwin comes to the door with his father and his brother. Now I get to hug him for the first time as I say good-bye. He is just a few inches shorter than I am, and I can fold my arms around him. I hold him tight, inhaling the mild scent of boyish sweat and bath soap. He shyly hangs on as long as I do.

He is laughing now and saying the odd phrases that he has picked up over the years from English cartoons. "What's up, doc?" he says as I go out the door.

"I'll be back tomorrow," I say as I go down the walk. Getting to know my youngest son again is going to take time. But it will be a labor of love.

In the following days, I find a job as a nurse's aide and rent an apartment. I spend most of my free time with Rodwin and Shadwin.

We go to the movies to see *Raiders of the Lost Ark.* Then we have ice cream at Baskin and Robbins. My sister Gail drives down to San Diego with her daughters and we all swim at La Jolla Cove. Both Rodwin and Shadwin are strong swimmers and love the ocean. We visit the Wild Animal Park and the San Diego Zoo. It's a perfect summer as far I'm concerned.

But over time, Mansoor starts to resent my presence. Now, he doesn't even come out of his bedroom when I visit. The boys serve fruit, candies, and soft drinks with their Persian flare for hospitality. Then, gradually, a change comes over them, too. I feel they are holding back, not hugging me when I arrive or leave. The hospitality slows to a trickle and then stops altogether. I don't care. I come to see them, not to eat or drink. When we are away from their father, they still act spontaneous and loving, so I don't worry about it.

It's now autumn, which doesn't mean much in Southern California—maybe a sweater in the morning. On my day off, I come to pick the boys up to go to Balboa Park. Rodwin answers the door as usual, but doesn't invite me in.

"My father and Shadi no longer live here," he tells me standing in the doorway.

I can't assimilate his words. They won't penetrate my head.

"Get Shadi, and let's go," I say as if I heard nothing amiss.

"They're gone."

"You mean for the day?"

"They've moved out of state, I'm living here alone." He looks so troubled that I want to ignore the burning pain in my throat. But I can't. I'm devastated.

"Mansoor doesn't want to see you again."

His words hit me like a physical blow. I lean against the doorpost for support. I should have seen it coming. He forbade them to even serve me a soft drink. Now I realize he must have given them a hard time every time we spent the day together. It's always about him, not their happiness.

"What about you, Rodwin? Do you want me out of your life?" I still can't digest what he means by *out of state*. So I concentrate on the immediate situation before me.

"I don't want you *or* my father in my life. I want to be alone." His voice is tight and strained.

The pain in his eyes hurts me more than his words. I know the words come from Mansoor. How could a father hurt his own children by making them choose between their parents?

"All right," I say weakly. "I'll leave you alone." I turn and walk away with a lead weight sitting on my chest. It feels like the oxygen has been sucked out of the universe. I don't need to breathe air. I'm a zombie, numb in body and spirit.

The hurt is so great that I can't discuss it with anyone, not even my mother or sisters. I also feel a deep sense of shame. Hot, searing shame that I don't measure up. My own children have rejected me. I'm not a good mother. All these years, I have deluded myself that I would have been the perfect mother, if only Mansoor would give me the chance.

Over the next days and weeks, I realize it is futile to try to track Mansoor down. If I find him, he will only disappear again. It's too late to gain legal custody of Shadwin. He will be fourteen on his next birthday. Any judge would ask him which parent he wants to live with. I won't force him to make a painful choice, knowing the odds are not in my favor.

I respond to my loss in the typical pattern I've observed over the past years. I make a major move. If I can't be a normal mother and lead a normal life, I will go back to Israel. In Israel, nothing is normal. There, every aspect of daily living is bigger than life. It's easy to lose myself in the violent upheaval of history in the making.

With money I saved while working as a nurse's aide in San Diego, I rent a house in Tiberias. This house, like most of the older dwellings in the Galilee, is made of black volcanic rock from the Golan.

The floors are laid with hand-painted ceramic tiles glazed to look like oriental carpets. My bedroom has a balcony that overlooks a fig tree, and I have a partial view of the sea with the Golan Heights in the distance. The living room is large enough to mount theatrical productions. The windows look out on a lemon tree.

The owner of the house is an Arab who lives in the United States. I pay my rent, one year in advance, to his lawyer in Haifa. It's cheap, only a hundred dollars a month, but I'm liable for any repairs.

The only people I know in this town are Shaul and Zahava. Beside their boys, *Barak* and *Raam*, Thunder and Lightning, they now have two daughters, *Tohar* and *Anavah*, Purity and Humility. Their way of using attributes to name their children reminds me of the Native Americans' naming process. If I could rename myself, I think it would be Mara, as in bitter wood.

I find it hard to adapt to the humidity in Tiberias. The Sea of Galilee is situated several hundred meters below sea level in what is known as the African Rift Valley. One day I'm walking slowly up the lane to my house. The least amount of exertion produces a copious amount of perspiration, so I take my time.

I see a small black puppy dart under the bushes near my house. I'm curious, so I try to coax the pup out of the bush. She refuses to come out, so I go inside. The next day, I see the tip of the pup's little white face. This time, I have a bit of cheese in my pocket. I place it on the sidewalk and move on.

Looking back I see her run out, grab the food, then run back to safety. I do this for several days. On the fourth day, she feels secure enough to take food from my hand. After she's gulped it down, I lift her into my arms.

She is dirty, with matted fur, even ticks. So I bathe her and trim her coat with manicure scissors. After I pull off the ticks, I flush them down the toilet. I name her Nessie, which means "miracle" in Hebrew. It's a miracle that I am willing to love again, even if it is only a stray mutt. That night, I put an old quilt on the floor for Nessie to sleep on. By morning, I find a warm furry ball crowding me on my pillow.

My money is running out and I have to find work. Again, I'm obliged to find something that won't displace a local citizen. So, I go seek advice from my friend.

"Sharona, why don't you ask for work at the Catholic Convent?" Zahava says while she is fixing supper. She styles her dark hair in bangs and a ponytail, making her look like a teenager, not the soon-to-be mother of five. I spend a lot of time with her. Shaul is not home during the day, so I make myself useful folding diapers, washing the dishes, or playing games with one of the older children.

"I didn't know there was a convent in Tiberias. Where?"

"Adjacent to the Scottish Hospice. We knew the cook before she went back to America."

"I'll go there first thing tomorrow."

The next morning, I pull on the bell rope. Two dogs on the other side of the wall rush to the unmarked convent gate, barking and snarling.

"Nelly! Missy! Calm down," says a voice over the wall.

Cautiously, I peek through the little window in the metal gate. "Do you need a cook?" I ask.

"It looks like our prayers are answered," a voice replies. An elderly, white-haired nun opens the gate and says she's Sister Olivet. Then she introduces me to the convent dogs, who now are wagging their tails. They look like vicious junkyard dogs, and I try to ignore them.

Sister Olivet leads me into the large living room of the three-story building. The room is cool and dark. "Sister Juliet, meet our new cook." She introduces me to a middle-aged woman. Neither wears the traditional nun's habit, but are dressed in conservative skirts and blouses.

"Our new program will begin soon," Sister Juliet explains. "Twenty-five nuns from Africa and Asia will come here to study the

Scriptures. We need someone to cook lunch and dinner, six days a week. Do you want the job?"

"Yes," I say at once. I have a good feeling about this place. If I'm an answer to their prayers, they have also answered mine.

Sister Juliet shows me the old-fashioned kitchen. "These two ancient gas stoves date back to the British Mandate. The pantry is stocked with canned goods, and the freezer holds a side of frozen beef imported from Argentina. Fresh fruit and vegetables, as well as dairy products and bread, come from the local market."

At first I feel anxious about cooking for people from such diverse backgrounds. The nuns from Korea and India like rice three times a day. Those from Africa prefer cornmeal. I prepare a basic American menu of meat, vegetables, salad, and dessert straight out of *The Joy of Cooking*. It's a big relief to find that nuns eat, without complaint, whatever is set before them.

Once a month they prepare a Sunday dinner based on their own national cuisine. One Sunday it's Filipino-style chicken smothered in garlic. Another Sunday, it's beef simmered in a peanut sauce over cornmeal mush, African style. The Koreans pickle jars of fermented raw vegetables, called *kimchi*. The Sister from Sri Lanka makes a red-hot curry using her own stash of spices and chili.

One afternoon, during the siesta period, a Sister from Ghana comes to the kitchen.

"Will you teach me to bake a cake?" she asks shyly.

"Do you want to bake for your convent when you return home?"

"No oven," she replies.

"You can bake on top of the burner with a homemade oven," I suggest.

"No burner, just charcoal fire," she answers.

Undeterred, I explain how to place an empty metal drum over an open fire.

"No flour, no sugar, no butter."

With new understanding, I help her make her first cake. We

beat the eggs, cream sugar, and pour the batter into the pan. Waiting for the cake to raise, we sit on the verandah looking out at the shimmering blue lake, trying to imagine what it was like two thousand years ago. How did the women who followed Jesus attend to the practical side of preparing meals?

Sunday mornings, the Sisters celebrate Mass in the little church of Saint Peter's, where the waves of the Sea of Galilee lap almost at the door. But on special feast days, Father Philip comes to the convent. The African Sisters, wearing traditional African robes and turbans, prepare a liturgy with drums and dancing. The nuns from Thailand, wearing delicate silk robes, set up the altar with garlands of flowers and baskets of fruit.

I feel at home here, though I'm the only salaried staff and not even a Catholic. Sister Mary Margaret greets me every morning with a warm hug. Sister Carmen, the Superior, is always the first one in the kitchen to help scrub the pots and pans.

One afternoon, Sister Mary Margaret comes into the kitchen and tells me to set another place for supper. "We have a visitor who's originally from South Bend," she tells me. I didn't know *South* Bend from *North* Bend before I started working here, but soon learned that the staff comes from Saint Mary's, which is part of Notre Dame University in South Bend, Indiana.

The visitor is tall, lean, and handsome. He wears a khaki shirt, shorts, and leather sandals. His hair touches his shirt collar and his skin is deeply tanned.

"What brings you to the Galilee?" Sister Carmen asks the visitor sitting at our table.

"I'm working a construction job on the Golan," he replies.

"How did you know we were here?"

"I didn't. I was looking for the Scottish Hostel when I rang your bell. Brother Ed came to the gate and recognized my Hoosier accent. And here I am eating dinner with you." Patrick smiles a broad smile. Everyone at the table smiles back, including me. I'm smitten with his eyes, the color of the Sea of Galilee at mid-day.

Sister Carmen, recognizing a good thing, invites Patrick to stay on as a volunteer. Brother Ed needs help trimming the orange trees, painting the bedrooms, and setting new tile in the chapel.

When Patrick has free time, he comes into the kitchen "just to talk." I sit on a stool beside the aluminum work table, chopping vegetables, pounding beef cutlets, or beating cake batter. He sits on a chair by the open door where he can pick up the breeze. It's hotter than blazes in the kitchen and there is only one fan, directly above me. Nellie, one of the convent dogs, is usually sleeping under my work table.

Patrick talks to me about his travels around Turkey and the four years he lived in Germany.

"Why did you come to Israel?" I ask.

"I wanted to see more than Turkey, but I didn't want to go back to Germany just yet," he replies.

I sense a kindred spirit. Someone who moves from place to place, country to country, like a bird whose natural habitat has been destroyed.

"So one day I took the ferry to Rhodes and caught the first boat leaving for Israel. In Haifa I heard about a job on the Golan, and the rest you know."

Emotions that I haven't felt in years surge up in my heart. I mentally check myself, refusing to allow even the possibility of romance. I'm through with men. Didn't I cut off my long hair when I turned forty? I had wanted to snip it all off with manicure scissors, making myself bald. I restrained myself though. A friend cut my hair above my ears. Now, at 42, in my shapeless cotton dress, full apron, and sturdy sandals, I don't feel attractive. Besides, he is younger than me.

The summer passes uneventfully. In the fall, Patrick returns to Germany. He sends me postcards about his hikes in the German Alps. I write him short notes about my life in Tiberias.

Then it's summer again, and he writes that he is coming back to the Galilee. The first night after dinner, Patrick and I walk out to the convent garden. I sit in the swing that hangs from the Jacaranda tree. The sun has set and the sea is cast in purple shadows. Fruit bats dart among the trees. The air is thick with the scent of orange blossoms.

I sense Patrick didn't come back to the Galilee only to help the nuns. There is a current of excitement between us, though neither of us acknowledges it.

"Marry me," Patrick says without preamble.

"Are you crazy?" I reply without looking at him. My mind is a whirl of conflicting emotions as I consider the ten-year age difference. At the same time I'm moved to tears that he has asked.

"Think about it," he says. "I believe God wants us to be together."

I look up with wonder. Could it be true?

"You know I never use His name lightly."

It's true. Patrick's faith is deep and sure, but not something he talks about, unlike most of my other Christian friends.

The second time he proposes, a week later, I say yes. I don't know if I'm following my heart or God's will. We kiss for the first time and he is such a good kisser that I think I'm going to swoon, like a heroine in a silent movie. We take the bus to Bethlehem to buy an engagement ring. I choose a small sapphire in a gold setting. Then we celebrate with a glass of wine at the King David Hotel. The pianist in the bar is playing the theme from *Doctor Zhivago* as we make a toast to our future.

Patrick wants a Catholic ceremony, even though I'm not a Catholic. I frankly don't care, one way or another. But it means I have to be interviewed by a church official to establish that I'm truly a baptized Christian. The Church will marry a non-Catholic with a Catholic, but only if the non-Catholic is a baptized Christian. But after considerable thought I decide to join the Catholic Church. The Sisters in Tiberias set such a sterling example that I had already revised my former, uninformed, notions about the Catholic faith.

To facilitate this change in status, I must be interviewed by two Franciscan monks who represent the Vatican in Jerusalem.

"I was baptized in the Holy Spirit in Teheran, then baptized some years later in a river in Waco, Texas," I tell them.

"Holy Spirit baptism?" One brown-robed monk turns to the other, with his palm up.

"You know, as in the first book of Acts," I add for clarification.

"Ah, of course, Pentecost." He nods in approval to his partner. "But about the water baptism. Was it done in the name of the Father, Son, and Holy Spirit?"

"I can't remember the exact words the preacher used."

"Was he from a traditional denomination? Baptist? Lutheran?"

"No, he was just a preacher passing through Waco. I don't believe he belonged to a denomination."

The Italian priests accept that I am Christian, but have doubts about the validity of the water baptism because the preacher had no denominational designation. Thus, I agree to be rebaptized by Father Philip in the little church of St. Peter's in Tiberias. Sister Ellen will be my catechist.

Their next question is, "Have you ever been married before?"

"Yes, I married a Muslim." I can see they are surprised.

"So, it was not a Christian marriage?"

"I guess not. He's a Muslim. At the time, I was an agnostic."

The wedding takes place six months later, on Patrick's birthday. We choose the Church of the Visitation, a historic Crusader Church that commemorates the meeting between Mary and Elizabeth, the mother of John the Baptist.

I wear a knee-length, beige silk dress and a tiny lace veil. Patrick wears a pair of borrowed dress pants and a white shirt. My Messianic friends fill the church with flowers and provide harp and guitar music. Father Philip preaches a sermon on the Virgin Mary that makes all the Jewish and Protestant guests feel uncomfortable. As he goes on and on, I hear the shuffling of feet and clearing of throats as their discomfort level rises.

During the reception, we cut the traditional wedding cake, as well as a birthday cake for Patrick. The big cake has three layers, with pink flowers. The little cake is chocolate. I help Patrick blow out his birthday candles, and he helps me cut the wedding cake.

The next morning, we sail on a ship bound for Turkey. Always a frugal traveler, Patrick arranges for us to sleep on the open deck. Not my idea of the perfect honeymoon, yet I'm happier than I ever dreamed possible.

In Turkey, we stay in caravansaries or guest houses as we travel around western Anatolia. When I first met Patrick, he owned one pair of trousers and two shirts. On the honeymoon, I find little is going to change. I buy new outfits in every bazaar. He purchases nothing, even though cotton goods are much cheaper in Turkey than in Israel. Like most new couples, we find we are opposites. He can go all day on a chocolate bar. I faint if I don't have three meals a day. He is zealous to explore every ruin and antiquity, a portent of things to come. I enjoy people watching.

Back in Israel, we find jobs with an American television station in Jerusalem that broadcasts in English and Arabic. We make friends with both Jews and Arabs. But after two years, we decide to return to America when the Palestinian uprising makes it impossible to travel freely in the West Bank. In 1989, I return to live in California, twenty-six years after I first left for Iran.

Epilogue

San Diego, 2001

My sons, now grown men, welcomed me back and quickly warmed to Patrick. I was delighted and humbled to find the bonds of love between mother and sons, though severely strained in the past, were not broken beyond repair.

Rodwin married an American girl. He and his wife now have two wonderful sons. Shadwin is also married now, and he and his wife have a daughter. Surely, God has restored the years eaten by the canker worm, as I hold these, my grandchildren, in my arms.

I finished the studies I dropped those many years ago when I eloped with Mansoor. The second time around, I was the same age as my professors, even older than some. I now have a BA in English Literature.

Patrick went back to the university to earn his Masters. As an archaeobotanist, his work now takes him, and me, back to the Middle East, back to my beloved Jerusalem.

Mansoor is living in seclusion somewhere in California.

My story is not over; there is much more to learn and do. To quote Saint Paul, "This one thing I do, forgetting those things which are behind, and reaching forth to those things which are ahead, I press toward the mark for the prize of the high calling."

I leave you, dear reader, with the same psalm that I quoted at the beginning of this story:

"We spend our years as a tale that is told."

About the Author

Sharon Geyer grew up in southern California, one of six children of a milkman and a homemaker. Nothing in Sharon's ordinary American upbringing would prepare her for the adventures and trials she experienced from 1963 to 1989, first in Iran and later in Israel. Those adventures are chronicled in her first book, *Daughter of Jerusalem: An American Woman's Journey of Faith*, which, as an unpublished manuscript entitled "Then Sings My Soul," was awarded first place for narrative nonfiction in the 2000 San Diego Book Awards.

Sharon returned to the United States with her husband Patrick in 1989 and subsequently earned a bachelor's degree in English literature from Arizona State University. She lives and writes today on a houseboat docked in San Diego Harbor, which she shares with her husband, an archaeobotanist and adjunct professor at the University of San Diego. She has written a mystery novel set in Iran and has begun work on a sequel to *Daughter of Jerusalem.*